Three Men and

First published by Rag D(

in 2010

Website: www.ragdollmediauk.com

Email enquiries:

ken.mcewan@talktalk.net

John Dowling mayflower39@btinternet.com

philip.elms@btinternet.com

ISBN 978-0-9565449-0-2

A catalogue record of this book is available
from the British Library.

Printed in Great Britain by impression IT

Unit 2, Maunsell Road,

St Leonards-on-Sea,

East Sussex TN38 9NL

Acknowledgements

WE warmly acknowledge the role of Robin and Pauline Thompson who cast a critical eye at the manuscript and offered valued advice.

We raise a glass to the hundreds of journalists, photographers, ad reps, printers and administrative staff who coloured our working lives for nearly half a century by offering good company, good humour, scepticism and sarcasm in equal measure.

We are grateful to Joan Harding for bringing some sanity to the table and to generations of newspaper readers for giving our careers true purpose.

We offer big thank-yous to author Victoria Seymour for encouragement and sound advice; John Davis at *impression IT* for personal involvement in the production of this book and *Waterstone's* for showing faith in the project.

We dedicate this book to our wives and families whose love and support has been out of all proportion to the nefarious demands of a fascinating, if slightly mad, industry.

Ken McEwan, John Dowling, Philip Elms

For Rag Doll Media UK

Stylisation and cover design: Philip Elms

Three Men photographs: Camilla Lake

Introduction

WHEN journalists give up the day job after a long career, people often ask: Are you going to write a book?

It happened to us. Each of us was inclined to respond: Who'd want to read it?

Then a deeper reality set in. To our horror, we realised we were sitting on nearly a century and a half of collective newspaper experience. To our delight, we realised we could create a permanent account of this.

It was not simply the high number of years involved. Rather, it dawned on us that our careers had started in the same era and in the same poky office of a small south coast weekly in Bexhill-on-Sea.

Equally, those careers were coming to an end simultaneously as the 2009 recession ripped hurricane-like through the regional press.

Having gone off at various tangents for more than four decades, circumstances conspired to send us through the same door marked Exit.

The idea emerged that each could give his own version of how it all started ... and finished.

In between we could explain how our different chosen strands of journalism propelled us through life, complete with personal influences, triumphs and tragedies, hobbies and interests and, not least, how our wives stuck by us throughout so patiently, yet so lovingly.

So could we conjure up that publishing rarity, a curiously-linked three-way autobiography? We were encouraged to think so, if only to illuminate our grandchildren.

As in those optimistic days of the 1960s when we first dipped our toes in the water, we were suddenly three men in the same boat again.

The title of our book seemed to flow naturally from there.

Ken McEwan   John Dowling   Philip Elms

Three quotes from the men

FREDDIE Goodsell was not the most conventional of editors. He was well known for his love of whisky and certainly enjoyed a nip or three during the working day. Whether he was due for one or had just indulged when I arrived for my first interview I don't know. But it lasted all of two minutes.

Ken McEwan

IMAGINE a hamster in its cage trotting on its little treadmill. Like the treadmill, newspaper production has no beginning and no end, instead a ceaseless demand to produce and process copy and pictures to feed its voracious appetite. For nearly half a century we three have been happy hamsters. This book, part history, part biography, part anecdote, may explain why.

John Dowling

IT'S probably no coincidence that my dual interests of newspapers and theatre have dovetailed so conveniently. The similarities are clear. One is a representation of real life, the other thinks it is but is really an illusion. The only issue is deciding which is which.

Philip Elms

Forewords

THESE are difficult times for the local newspaper industry. The dual forces of a recession and the ever-accelerating 'digital revolution' have conspired to cut editorial staffing to basic survival levels. It is an appropriate time, therefore, to look back on better times when editorial excellence really mattered and when the loyalty and accumulated knowledge of long-serving journalists was prized by proprietors.

The authors of this book have made an immeasurable contribution, each in his own way, to the coverage of news and sport in East Sussex, and I count it a privilege to have known Phil, Ken and John for nearly 44 years.

Their memoirs will be eagerly anticipated by all who have ridden the rollercoaster of local newspaper journalism since the 1960s, and will fascinate many who have read their Observers, Herald or Express down the years in blissful ignorance of the sweat and tears often shed by those in the editorial engine room.

Peter Austin (former weekly editor and managing director)

AS a reporter, no two working days are the same – that's the great attraction. Another feature is that in every newsroom up and down the country you will find colourful characters. So even on a slow news week, office life is often a huge entertainment with smart, witty comments peppering the day, hilarious impressions of interviewees, and a fair few stand-up rows and hissy fits.

I have worked closely for many years alongside Philip Elms at Hastings, while also liaising with John Dowling at the Bexhill "outpost" over joint stories. They are true sages of the local newspaper world to whom I could turn for advice or a second opinion on any awkward issue. Along with Ken McEwan, they are wise old owls of the business, matured well like a good red wine, but still just as excited by an exclusive scoop as when they were cub reporters.

Dependable and trustworthy, they are from the solid, decent brigade of reporters and editors, which sometimes seems to be fast disappearing. *Three Men and a Quote* provides quite an eye-opener as to what really goes on. It is the ultimate newspaper supplement.

Sandra Daniels
East Sussex journalist

THREE Men and a Quote is the beguiling story behind the unsung heroes of regional newspapers. To many Philip Elms, Ken McEwan and John Dowling epitomised the devotion and craft of regional newspaper journalism; tireless in their pursuit of excellence – and most of all, a bloody good story. They were the guardians of truth and loyal servants to their districts.

As group commercial editor and later associate editor I enjoyed a charming working relationship with Elmo and often admired his composure when the pressure gauge hissed (which it invariably did). The consummate professional, Elmo will always be a gentleman of integrity – and a stickler for detail. I cut my journalistic teeth under the watchful specs of Ken McEwan and I can think of no better training ground. A more tenacious and assiduous journalist you will never meet.

Quite frankly, what Elmo, Mac and JD didn't know about their patches – well, no-one else did. Notably, during the relentless charge of new media, none lost his poise. These stalwarts kept their pencils sharp to the very end, collecting some heart-warming and uproarious anecdotes on the way.

Three Men and a Quote is a compelling triography of three venerable local journalists who bled ink for more than four decades.

Andrew Bennett
East Sussex and Essex journalist

WE are all used to headlines screaming at us from both the national and local media. *Three Men and a Quote* is the personal story behind the headlines that is a compelling read not just for those people living in the area it is set. It charts the beginning, middle and end of three men's working lifetime in which they show true dedication and loyalty to their craft.

The changing face of newsgathering from broadsheet to tabloid is told in their own different and inimitable style. The highs, the lows, the tragedies and the happy times are laid bare. *Three Men and a Quote* is a fascinating true life story – you couldn't make it up if you tried.

Gill Miller
East Sussex journalist

IF you have ever wondered what goes on behind the scenes of your local newspaper, then *Three Men And A Quote* is the book for you. John Dowling, Philip Elms and Ken McEwan all hung up their notebooks in 2009 after spending their entire working lives in the local Press.

Their stories make fascinating reading, especially as each chose to take a different tack in the world of journalism: John – Mr Bexhill – the consummate reporter, Ken a sporting institution with his opinion column and Phil a production editor with a keen eye for accuracy and a sharp headline.

Not only is this book a peek behind the scenes, it is a milestone in a world where the newspaper industry is facing immense change due to financial pressures and technological revolution. It is both revealing and poignant.

Julia Northcott
East Sussex journalist

A personal tribute

NOSTALGIA'S a great thing - as long as it isn't removed from reality so that the only people to smile are the stars of the story. When people in the media speak of the Good Old Days, I often look at the culture of the old newsrooms, the content of the pages, the personality of the key players, the response of the local community.

And within a few seconds I feel real nostalgia - and join the chorus of criticism of the decline in the local and provincial Press in the last 20 years. I worked alongside people who had ink in their veins. They had one thing in common: The need to inform the public - *their* public - of stories that mattered in a way that was clear, objective and stimulating. At least that was the aim. And they didn't look at the clock. Or the balance sheet. Or even the bottom line of the weekly pay slip.

They were men - and women - whose vocational impetus was to inform, to stimulate, to make a potent link between the source and the street. Nothing else was important. They even had to find partners who agreed to come second when the news broke, especially on deadline. This book features three such media monsters. And their tale charts about 50 years of life in the streets of East Sussex.

I arrived here in 1986 to take over the world's foremost editorial training operation for Westminster Press. We were based on two floors of Marina Court in St Leonards. Then as now, JOHN DOWLING was arguably the best known man in Bexhill. His name became synonymous, for me and for the hundreds of leading journalists and broadcasters who were trained here, with the big news story of the week on Page One. But then came Page 2, and 3 and 4, and 26 and 27. Still the man's name stood over stories about his beloved patch. We wondered in fact whether he was three journalists working under the same by-line! But no, he was real alright - and a more unassuming giant never graced a newsroom.

PHILIP ELMS, on the other hand, was invisible - despite his more robust proportions! And it was his larger-than-life personality that shone through the pages of the Observer. Any old school newsman will tell you that without the right packaging there is a danger that the best stories will be lost in poor design.

Like all great chief sub-editors - or whatever they're called these days - Elms presided over the 40-odd years of news and feature stories. His art was to do all he could to spot the key elements that would make each item sparkle ... and wait for the moment when the story was so big he could smile and relax before going into the attack - knowing he could afford to use a scalpel rather than a mallet. It's ironic that often the greatest power in a newspaper is, like Elms, never seen, or known. This book is his chance to come from the shadows and take his proper place.

Philip can recall how often in this sports-mad area, the Back Page becomes the Front Page. And KEN McEWAN, a journalist at the centre - and usually the cutting-edge - of the big East Sussex sports stories over the last 40 years, was normally responsible. Bobby Moore, Ron Greenwood, Jimmy Greaves and Martina Navratilova ... the stars of yesterday stand alongside all the emerging stars in his notebook. And amid the power-packed headlines are the endless controversies over players starring, winning and cheating. And above all, Mac shines the light on all the hundreds of unsung heroes who, like him, give their hearts to the growth of sport in this area, sometimes at great personal cost.

He reminds us that it isn't the great news break that makes Mac - or Dowling or Elms - so special. It's the absolute commitment to providing a weekly digest of all that's important against sometimes forbidding obstacles of time, money and myriad commercial pressures.

All three have managed to avoid bitterness over the decline of standards, of newspapers, of profit, or credibility, as the multi-media revolution substitutes speed for depth, global for local, quantity for quality, superficial entertainment for intelligent and balanced coverage. These men belonged to an era when they would have worked for nothing to get the job done. Maybe they would say they did!

Thanks to them - and all those who sustained the local Press and kept communities functioning better in what now appear to be better days. We will not see their like again.

ROBIN THOMPSON

Ex-evening and weekly newspaper editor

Who's Where

Three Men and a Quote
Part 1

The Ken McEwan Story

KEN McEwan was born in London on October 25th, 1944, with the Second World War still raging. At the tender age of six months his family brought him to St Leonards where it was considered safer - only for a bomb to fall on the beach just 100 yards from the Seaside Road home where baby Ken, tucked away in a chest of drawers - was now living with his parents, grandparents and elder sister Joan. Ken entered journalism at the age of 15, leaving Hastings Grammar School to become a junior reporter on the Bexhill-on-Sea Observer. He was appointed chief reporter at the age of 19 and two years later was given his first sports editor's job on the Kent Messenger-owned Tonbridge Free Press. Two months before England won the World Cup, Ken accepted an invitation to edit the sports pages of the Hastings & St Leonards Observer, a position he held for 13 years. He switched to the Eastbourne Gazette & Herald as sports editor in 1979, being promoted to assistant editor (news and sport) in 1987. He returned to his original role as full-time sports editor in 1996. With the recession forcing Johnston Press to restructure its editorial staff, Ken took voluntary retirement eight months early in February, 2009, but continues to cover football for the Gazette & Herald and the national Non League Paper. His retirement came after nearly 49 years in the newspaper industry, just on 30 at Eastbourne. Ken married Kathy in February 1975, when he also adopted her three children, Roger, Angela and Richard. His family was happily extended by the birth of Kevin in 1980 and Karen three years later. He lives at Hastings.

1 A £10 suit – and a two-minute interview

IT was the most expensive acquisition of my young life, a brand new suit costing £10 saved from my hard-earned paper round money.

A knock on the door from my next door neighbour started it all. Mrs Lamont knew I wanted to be a newspaper reporter and spotted an advert for a junior in the Hastings Observer.

I wasn't over-optimistic. I was 15, planned to go back to school for another year and hoped to establish myself in the Hastings Grammar School 1st XI football team.

Long gone were my ambitions to become a professional footballer. I was vice-captain of the grammar school under-15s but I no longer felt I had the potential to earn a living at the game I loved.

So if I couldn't achieve a career in professional football, surely I could do the next best thing – write about it.

I penned a letter to the Hastings Observer editor and was over the moon when I received one back inviting me for an interview.

Freddie Goodsell was not the most conventional of editors. He was well known for his love of whisky and certainly enjoyed a nip or three during the working day. Whether he was due for one or had just indulged when I arrived for my interview I don't know.

But it lasted all of two minutes.

"So why do you want to be a reporter on the Observer?" was the one question I remember.

"It has for a long time been my ambition to report on the happenings of Hastings," was the best reply I could come up with.

A brief explanation about the job and the interview was over.

The inevitable letter of rejection arrived the next day. I discovered later that Goodsell had already made his choice – a young man by the name of Bill Hay.

What a waste of £10 – or so I thought. A week later a second letter arrived, signed by Leonard J. Bartley, editor of the Bexhill-on-Sea Observer.

My original application had been passed onto him and suddenly I was making my way, complete with (almost) new suit to the Western Road offices of the Observer.

After my first experience I was a little apprehensive to say the least.

But LJB was a different kettle of fish to Freddie Goodsell. The interview lasted about an hour and a half and finished with those unforgettable words – "I think you are the young man I have been looking for."

I left the office walking on air.

At the tender age of 15 I was in full-time employment having secured the job I desperately wanted. I was to be paid the princely sum of three pounds, six shillings and sixpence (£3-1-1d after tax).

Yes, I would need £1 a week for my train fare to Bexhill and back to Hastings.

Yes, I would need £1 a week for shorthand lessons from Miss Peirce who lived just around the corner from the Observer's Western Road office in Parkhurst Road.

And yes, I would be giving my mum £1 a week for my keep.

But hey, I had entered the profession of my choice and could say goodbye to school and a round of GCE exams.

Tuesday, August 2nd, 1960 was to become a red letter day in my life.

It was the day I started a journalistic career on the Bexhill-on-Sea Observer. Prime Minister Harold Macmillan was right. I had never had it so good.

2 Silent panic

TO say I was nervous on my first day would be an enormous understatement. The Old Man, as the editor was universally known in the office, tried to put me at ease. "We have all been through exactly what you are going through," he unsuccessfully reassured me. "We've all had a first day."

But then came a warning. "It's a busy office, so it's a case of sink or swim. You won't always find me easy to work for but in 10 years' time you'll thank me" – words I was to discover later that would certainly come true.

I soon got to know the rest of the staff – a sub-editor, three other reporters and a photographer.

"Stay on the right side of the Old Man and you'll be all right," warned photographer Jimmy Burke.

I was introduced to an ageing sub-editor, Bob Quayle, chief reporter Ken Hamer and reporters David Symington and Tony Tubb. I was amazed to see Tony who, at the age of 24, had started his journalistic career only a few months before me.

I had marvelled at his soccer trickery as he helped Bexhill Town win the county league championship despite having had a pain-killing injection for a chipped bone in his foot. He had gone on to become a professional footballer for my home club of Hastings United but had not been retained due to persistent injury problems.

I shadowed Tony on a couple of jobs on my opening week, firstly to a local rabbit show and then a bowls tournament.

But during my second week came my first moment of horror. I accompanied Ken Hamer to a sitting of the local valuation court where house-owners have the right to appeal against the rateable value of their property.

Ken busily took notes of the first case and then that heart stopping moment. "I have got to go on to another job. I'll leave you to do the rest. I know you haven't got shorthand yet, but just get down the important points."

That one instruction resulted in my heart skipping two beats. I was in silent panic as I somehow managed to reply, "I'll do my best."

I just about understood the remaining two cases and wrote stories for the paper. Nobody complained so I reckoned I had just about cleared my first serious hurdle.

As the week progressed I grappled with what seemed a thousand flower show results and at the weekend finally relaxed when I was sent to report on an Adam Faith concert at the De La Warr Pavilion.

Week three, however, provided a moment of good fortune. I pulled off my first scoop. I was with Jimmy Burke covering a run-of-the-mill garden party at Sidley when a runaway horse raced past.

"Come on," insisted Jimmy, "This is going to be a good story."

When we eventually caught up with the horse, it had been captured by a brave passer-by and a shaken rider was soon back in control.

I interviewed both passer-by and rider and obviously impressed the vastly experienced Jimmy Burke. We returned to the office and I started to write my story.

Jimmy, a hugely talented photographer with a nose for news, was not renowned for his compliments. He was, to say the least, a bit of a moaner. So I was immensely relieved when I heard him tell the editor: "I think we're got a useful reporter here. Mac asked all the right questions."

I knew, however, that I still had a lot to learn. But at least I seemed to be on the right road.

There have been numerous eventful weeks over the last 48 years, but the opening three on the Bexhill Observer remain etched in my memory. And Tony Tubb remains a best friend to this present day.

3 From office junior to chief reporter

AS my weeks progressed on the Bexhill Observer, I started to settle into a routine; every Monday morning a trip to the undertakers, (Mummery's and Longley & Co) to check the deaths of the previous seven days.

I would then report back to the Old Man and he would decide whether to send a form to the next of kin for them to fill in obituary details or, if he or she was well known, I would visit the bereaved relatives personally to get an in-depth report of the deceased.

I was also given the weekly task of reporting the luncheon meetings of the Bexhill branch of the National Council of Women, by which time I had reached the ripe old age of 16. I introduced myself to the organiser. "You are very young, aren't you?" was her immediate reply. But I would use my newly learned shorthand as best I could as I took down the highlights of the after-lunch speech before returning to the office to write my story.

I got used to being the only young man among numerous women. But that was nothing to what lay ahead. One weekend at the De La Warr Pavilion was scheduled the annual conference of the East Sussex Federation of Women. Some 800 women gathered from the east of the county with just one young male reporter in their midst – no prizes for guessing who.

My first milestone at Bexhill came in the sixth month. Ken Hamer left to join the Argus and a new junior was recruited by the name of John Woodland.

That was good news for me. I lost the routine jobs such as obituary calls and wedding write-ups. I had taken my first step up the journalistic ladder.

I have mentioned obit calls, but in those days we attended the big funerals, taking names of all those attending to include in our report. One notable funeral was attended by our own big white chief, Frederick J. Parsons, (FJ Parsons who then owned the Hastings and Bexhill Observers).

FJ was based at Hastings, but paid us regular visits invariably strutting around looking very important and smoking a large cigar. When he turned up at the church entrance where John and I were busily taking names, there was obviously no need to ask his. Or was there? John hadn't a clue who FJ was and was met with a gruff "FJ Parsons" when asked the embarrassing question. John, however, wanted to be in no doubt. "How do you spell that?" FJ glared and stormed off into the church.

It was clear as time went on that John was struggling – far more than me. He seemed to improve, but it was not enough for LJB. When John took his summer holiday, he received a letter saying he need not return to work.

Into the fray, in the summer of 1961, came another John who was to last somewhat longer than his predecessor. Somewhat longer? A lot longer – his name was John Dowling, a name that was to feature prominently in the community of Bexhill for nearly five decades.

John joined at a good time. As a result of a new wage agreement negotiated by the National Union of Journalists, we suddenly found that our weekly wage was doubled – to the tune of a huge £6 a week with eight weeks back pay. I immediately spent my bonanza on a down payment for a new motor scooter which put to shame the office Vespa - the equivalent of today's pool car.

I started to really enjoy life at Bexhill, but a lot of hard work lay ahead. David Symington left to join the Daily Mail and, at the age of 18, I suddenly found myself second in command to Tony Tubb who had been appointed chief reporter.

Mistakes are part and parcel of every newspaper. Reports are often turned out under pressure with deadlines looming. As the Old Man had pointed out, if a shopkeeper gives the wrong change, it is between him and the customer; if we make one, the whole world – or so it seems – gets to know.

My first error was an especially serious one – it affected one of the Old Man's cronies. I cannot recall her name, but she was due to be presented to the Queen Mother for a special award and I said she was presented to the Queen.

She created hell, claiming I had ruined her day, and I was subjected to a severe Old Man reprimand.

But even that seemed nothing to the hard time he gave sub editor Bob Quayle, a mild-mannered man in his fifties who seemed to wear the same overcoat year after year and had an annoying habit of re-writing virtually every story he dealt with.

Subbed stories were despatched to Hastings where the paper was then printed. We wrote the stories, the editor would decide their prominence on a given page and Quayle would sub them,

They would then be returned to the editor who would invariably complain to Quayle either about the quality of the headline or why he had rewritten perfectly good copy.

When LJB was ill, I would have to take Quayle's subbed copy to the Old Man's home where, coughing away in his dressing gown, he would check every word. In most instances he would send me back with notes demanding that Quayle restore re-written copy to its original form.

It was all quite bizarre and a relief to us all when FJ Parsons transferred Quayle to the Sussex Express and brought in Roy Jones (sports editor at Hastings) to replace him

Tony Tubb and I would report meetings of the Bexhill Town Council – meetings that would go long into a Wednesday night. The Old Man would also be there, taking his own notes and often comparing them with ours. We were expected to report debates in the same style as Hansard, the parliamentary bible. The Old Man would tell us what stories he would want for that week's Observer and we would start handwriting our reports, first in a pub and then in the Continental Club, on the seafront, usually well into the early hours of Thursday morning.

Our reward came at the end of the year when FJ would hold a giant Christmas party, for staff at Hastings, Bexhill and

Folkestone. The entire White Rock Pavilion would be taken over for a night of dancing, cabaret and a cold turkey buffet with a free bar for the entire evening. A fleet of buses would be laid on to take everyone home, having picked them up earlier in the evening. It was a wonderful night which did not cost anybody a penny.

All too soon, however, it was back to the grind and one day, came a shock to the system. Tony Tubb gave in his notice and moved to the Worthing Herald where he stayed for a week before moving onto the Southampton Evening Echo.

I assumed a new chief reporter would be appointed from outside. I had already been given the responsibility of producing the sports pages but the Old Man called me into his office and put to me a loaded question. "You don't really want me to advertise for a new chief reporter do you?"

I dread to think how he would have reacted had I said yes. The upshot was that I was made chief reporter at the age of 19 for a princely £10 a week (£5 less than the minimum senior rate). But I was given a regular weekly expense allowance of 10 shillings!

4 The big names

VARIETY is certainly the spice of life when working in provincial newspapers. As the Old Man reminded me during my five years at Bexhill – be prepared to meet anyone from a dustman to a government minister.

How right he was. During a short spell with the Kent Messenger I was sent out to do a full page feature on the day in the life of a dustman (these days refuse collectors of course), while at Bexhill I came into direct contact with the likes of the controversial Labour politician Anthony Wedgwood Benn, Tory Cabinet minister Sir Keith Joseph and the former Liberal leader Joe Grimond.

I have never been particularly politically motivated, but I was genuinely moved by a fighting speech from Tony Benn at a pre-general election meeting of the local Labour Party.

Predictably Benn hammered the ruling Conservative Party who were coming to an end of 12 years of government, ridiculing Harold McMillan's famous phrase "You have never had it so good."

Even as a 17-year-old reporter, I felt sufficiently moved to congratulate Benn on a brilliant fighting speech. "Coming from the press, that is quite something," he replied.

More big names came my way when I moved full-time into the world of sport. At an East Sussex Sports Association dinner at Hastings, I was privileged to be seated next to England soccer captain Bobby Moore, just a couple of weeks before he led the country's national team into world cup combat in Mexico.

Unbelievably, just days prior to the start of the tournament, Moore was to be arrested for stealing a £600 bracelet from a shop in his hotel in Bogota, Columbia, in what was obviously an attempt to frame one of the most honest and 'true gentleman' players ever to lead England.

It was a delightful evening with Bobby and his first wife Tina. How tragic that a great player, capped 108 times for England, should finally be beaten by cancer at the age of 52.

Perhaps my most moving big-name interview was with Jimmy Greaves, one of England's most prolific goal-scorers who I once saw net five times for England against Scotland at Wembley.

Jimmy was in Eastbourne launching his new book 'Greavesie.' I was struck not only by his dry sense of humour but by the obvious courage, not just in scoring goals for fun at national and international level, but his determination in beating what has got the better of so many of his counterparts over the years – the bottle.

His addiction to alcoholism virtually destroyed his life in latter years and his success in overcoming it was probably his greatest achievement. It was strange, back in the late seventies, to see this great man performing for Barnet against the likes of Hastings in the Southern League – where the FA Cup started in the preliminary round – after his European glory nights playing for Spurs at White Hart Lane.

It was the biggest name of all, however, who provided me with what I like to call my mini world scoop.

Martina Navratilova ruled women's tennis for two decades. She won the pre-Wimbledon tennis championships at Eastbourne 11 times and was worshipped at Devonshire Park. It was around five years ago when speculation was rife about her 'final' retirement. She first announced her retirement in 1994, but her special love of Eastbourne saw her back at Devonshire Park many more times. But at a press conference the great lady seemed to dodge all questions as to when her last game in Sussex would be.

Out of the blue I bumped into her during tennis week on the approach to Eastbourne railway station. "Are we going to see you playing here again?" I asked casually. "Not as a singles player," she replied emphatically. "I might return for the odd doubles match, but I have played my last match here as a singles player."

That fairly short conversation provided me with an excellent back page lead story and other papers followed it up. Martina had unwittingly given the game away – not realising she was speaking to a sports journalist.

5 Lucky to escape a night in the cells

AFTER five years at Bexhill it seemed time to move on. In short, I had really had enough of testing my shorthand to the limit during endless town council meetings.

When I spotted an advert in the Daily Mail for a sports editor on the Kent Messenger's Tonbridge Free Press I wasted no time in putting pen to paper.

The interview lasted the best part of two hours, including the laying out of a mock page, and KM deputy editor Dennis Fowler gave me no clues at the end of it. "I am interviewing for the rest of today and all day tomorrow" were his parting words.

I was overjoyed at getting a job advertised in a national newspaper. But first, there was a double celebration, my combined farewell and 21st birthday. It was a party never to be forgotten, mostly for the wrong reasons.

Staged at the Bo-Peep, a small, homely pub in St Leonards-on-Sea, it was attended by family, friends and colleagues from Bexhill. The drink flowed well into the early hours when a major problem arose. Colleague John Liddle was virtually out for the count after a night of heavy drinking. He had arrived in his dad's new car with a promise that it would be returned that evening.

Needless to say, John was in no state to drive home. So a bizarre contingency plan was put into action.

My brother-in law Jacques Bruno agreed to drive John back to Sidley in his dad's car. Jacques had no idea of the way and John was in no fit state to direct him so he would follow me, driving my brother-in-law's car accompanied by my sister Joan.

After delivering John and car back home, Jacques would drive Joan and I back to Hastings in his own car. It all made sense, apart from a few frightening facts.

I was still an inexperienced, inefficient learner driver never having driven Jacques' car before. I would be uninsured and driving without L plates – as well as having had far too much to drink.

But the drunken John was repeatedly heard to mumble "Must get my dad's car home" so there seemed no alternative. We set off, me with just a couple of months' dubious driving experience, heart beating rapidly, with Jacques and drunken John in the car behind.

I glanced in the mirror and spotted another car behind them. There was no mistaking it – that was definitely a police car following us.

I feared the worst as my blood pressure rapidly rose – a night in the cells, a hefty fine, banned from driving and goodbye to my new job. It was 3am and my worst nightmare was being played out in real life.

We finally arrived at Sidley. My driving inexperience showed as I scraped the car wheels against the kerb while pulling up outside John's house.

But mission had been accomplished and what a relief. The police car continued on its way, the two uniformed occupants obviously unaware they had been tailing a driver who had been breaking three laws in one fear-filled journey.

Me? I breathed my heaviest ever sigh of relief.

I cannot say that my short spell with the Tonbridge Free Press was the best period of my life. I lived in digs and hated it. There was no bypass in those days and driving through Tonbridge High Street could take anything up to an hour during busy periods.

In addition to covering Tonbridge Football Club whose manager, former Hastings United defender Harry Haslam went on to boss Luton Town, I had to plan the sports pages and cover a considerable amount of general news. It was county court every Tuesday and a general piece – including getting up at 5am for the dustman feature – at the end of the week.

In the office was a genuinely nasty chief sub-editor, talented at his job, but criticising everyone and everything just about every day.

He was intolerable, wanting every page to look like The Sun - not possible in a local newspaper trying to squeeze in as many local news items as possible.

One day I could stand no more. He called me to his desk to make a needless criticism of a particularly trivial matter.

In a fit of pique I swept, with one devastating blow of the hand, every paper on his desk to the floor, including subbed and unsubbed copy and page plans which had originally been in neat piles.

I then stormed into general manager Eric Maskell's office to say I could no longer work with him.

Maskell sympathised, saying he had met more reasonable people in charge when he was a prisoner-of-war, adding that with any luck that particular sub would be leaving soon.

Later that day, the sub-editor (I cannot recall his name) came up to me and warned: "I can be a good friend but a very bad enemy. You will soon find that out."

Fortunately, I never got to find out what those words actually meant. He was taken ill that night and was subsequently transferred to head office at Maidstone. I never saw him again.

It was a huge relief when I received a call from John Cornelius, the new editor of the Hastings Observer, inviting me to return to my home town as sports editor.

Chris Jones had quit the Observer and Cornelius was ready to offer me senior terms three years early (usually applicable at 24 years of age) as well as a free trip to Holland on a sports exchange later that year. It would be my third rise within a year.

Easter was approaching. "If you are interested why don't we have a chat over a drink," suggested Cornelius who lived on St Leonards seafront. "I can see you on Good Friday morning. Meet me at the Bo-Peep."

6 Coming home

SIX years after lasting two minutes as a 15-year-old interviewee, I found myself invited to join the Hastings Observer as sports editor. When new editor John Cornelius asked me when I could start, it was music to my journalistic ears.

It meant I could cover my beloved Hastings United, a club I had supported so avidly as a schoolboy during its most famous years. I was with my dad at the Pilot Field in December 1953 when little United thrashed mighty Swindon Town 4-1 to reach the third round proper of the FA Cup. United made mincemeat of their Football League opponents by sheer quality football and I shall never forget the scenes at the final whistle when crowds surged onto the pitch to mob their heroes.

The next round brought an even bigger fish to fry. As a hugely excited 10-year-old I was among the record 12,527 at the Pilot Field to watch United take on Norwich City.

The result is history – the game ended in a 3-3 draw but if ever a team should have gone through at the first time of asking it was United. Centre-forward Sid Asher missed a penalty, Norwich cashed in on a shocking Ray Barr passback to score and, in the closing minutes, George Peacock hit the underside of the crossbar.

United fully deserved to win a tremendous game but went down in the replay at Carrow Road 3-0.

Had they gone through, Hastings would have faced Arsenal at Highbury in the fourth round and, just to add insult to Hastings' injury, Norwich defeated Arsenal 2-1 on an icy pitch that was a great leveller. Would Hastings have done the same? I honestly think so.

When I arrived at the Pilot Field for the first time as sports editor of the Observer, another exciting chapter in the club's history was unfolding. Former Spurs star Bobby Smith had signed for the club just two years after turning out for England.

His wage was reputed to be £65 a week and he treated us to some classic goals, His first game at Ashford was greeted by TV cameras and a near 3,000-strong crowd, four times the normal figure.

But it was all about to turn sour. Smith failed to turn up for training sessions and to the disappointment and anger of more giant-sized crowds, he started to miss matches even when his name was on the team sheet. A derisory groan would break out among the fans when the replacement for Smith was announced over the loudspeaker with flu the most popular excuse. The burly centre-forward was suspended once by United and twice by the FA and finally his contract was terminated for failing once again to turn up for training.

United continued to produce amazing stories and characters. I was at Wealdstone in 1974 when the team actually walked off the field as a protest after conceding three penalties in the first half. Only after the desperate persuasion of chairman Keith Wratten did player-manager John Ripley agree to take his players back on the field for more action, eventually losing 5-2.

The seventies saw a constant period of managerial change. Two great characters to occupy the managerial chair were the former Portsmouth centre-half Reg Flewin and the ex-England under-23 captain Peter Sillett.

Flewin arrived at the Pilot Field on £40 a week and was determined to earn his money in more ways than one. I would often call round to find him scrubbing his office floor, such was his dedication to the cause. He was finally sacked by chairman Keith Wratten as "a luxury the club could no longer afford". But Flewin gave me a great exclusive story by revealing that after being shown the door by Wratten three directors had invited him out to lunch with the sole intention of persuading him to stay on. Wratten was left angry and embarrassed, but the end result was what he wanted – Flewin went.

Sillett, however, seemed to take the job less seriously and would invariably be seen drifting out of the club bar midway during a second half having missed several goals. Sometimes, it seemed, pints were as important as points. However, he went on to take United to the third round of the FA Trophy. But Sillett always had a smile on his face in in the boardroom after defeat, hating the thought of the opposition thinking his feelings had been hurt.

But it was the arrival of Bobby Drake to the Pilot Field that presented me with what I will always regard as my greatest story – although neither Hastings United nor their supporters would be likely to agree!

7 German divers and a wedding ring

COMING home to Hastings had many benefits, not least an annual European adventure to either Germany or Holland. In the little village of Illerzell, West Germany, the Hastings youth soccer team would represent England against 'international' opposition such as Italy, Belgium and France.

It was a momentous experience.

On the opening day of the tournament, the teams would march through the village, led by the local brass band.

For five days, group matches would take place in true world cup fashion culminating in the play-off for third place and grand final.

The Hastings squad would stay with German players and I was hosted by the village band leader, his wife and two teenage daughters. At the end of each day there was a grand beer festival staged under giant marquees.

Between games there were periods of relaxation and that was when I came a bit of a cropper.

It was May, 1975, just three months after I had married Kathy. There were no games scheduled for a sunny Tuesday morning and I got involved in a bizarre game of hand tennis – in the sea. I was having the time of my life until a sudden realisation. My three-month old wedding ring was missing.

In panic I alerted others. Within 10 minutes a team of at least four German divers, complete with breathing gear, were underwater searching for my ring.

Sadly they were unsuccessful, but their gallant efforts were a measure of the magnificent German hospitality we enjoyed throughout our five-day visit.

Of course I still had to go home and break the news of the missing wedding ring to Kathy. Being the wonderful girl she was (and still is), she did not complain – and within days had bought me a replacement.

The big story from the trip was that Hastings actually won the tournament. They were presented with a magnificent trophy though I felt it was unfortunate that they did not bring home any medals. It would have been a lasting memento of a stunning triumph.

I wrote a comment piece for the Observer pointing this out and was accused in an angry letter from the Hastings organisers of leaving a sour taste in the mouths of our hosts back in Germany.

It was pointed out in the letter that the boys themselves did not want medals. They were sufficiently happy with the honour of winning.

So I went to see the Hastings skipper, Kevin Barry, who confirmed to me that they would dearly loved to have brought home medals.

I fired a letter off to the organisers letting them know in no uncertain terms the views of the captain. A humble letter of apology was my reward.

In Dordrecht there was rarely controversy, just a week of games and activities including tennis, table tennis, judo and ballroom dancing.

I would stay with a Dutch journalist and report on the games, telephoning my piece back to Hastings on the Thursday for inclusion in that Saturday's paper.

I was also invited to write a column for De Dordtenaar, the Dordrecht evening paper which gave the week blanket coverage. It was translated by the sports editor into Dutch.

It was all good, clean fun with Hastings and Dordrecht taking turns as hosts with a grand farewell party bringing each week to a memorable conclusion.

Hastings later became twinned with Dordrecht largely, I would imagine, as a result of the sports exchange which took place over many years and organised at the Hastings end by former water polo international Denys Lock who sadly died in 2008.

8 Breaking the rules

IT'S a question I am often asked – what was the biggest story I have ever covered? The answer is immediate. It was the story which knocked Hastings United out of the FA Trophy.

Officially, United were thrown out of the competition and fined £100 for fielding an ineligible player against Maidstone United in 1977. But the drama goes much deeper than that.

It all started when a sharp-eyed compositor by the name of Roger Smith was making up the Hastings Observer sports pages on a Thursday afternoon.

Roger was a keen United fan and, like many of the Observer's soccer-mad printers, was keen to read all the sports news in advance of publication day.

There were two reports he was avidly reading - a goalless draw at Maidstone on the Saturday and a 2-0 Tuesday night replay win at the Pilot Field which had earned United a plum home draw in the next round against Slough.

Roger got to the end of the Saturday report and the publication of the United team and pointed out to me: "You've got the goalkeeper's name wrong here."

All I knew was that, because of injury, United had fielded their reserve keeper, a player they named as Micky Hayward. I did not watch the reserves so accepted the information in good faith.

I telephoned manager Bobby Drake to find out just who the mystery keeper was. He would not tell me. He pleaded with me to go along with the name that appeared in my report.

I told him I would never knowingly print anything that I knew to be untrue. It was his job to tell me the truth. Otherwise I would write a story querying the name.

Drake set about plan B.

It was ironic that he lived next door to editor Peter Welham. The two were not only neighbours but firm friends, regularly joining each other for Sunday lunch. "Peter will support me," insisted Drake. "He would never publish a story like that."

But Drake was to get no joy out of the editor who immediately scented a front page story. So who was the mystery keeper? That was the question I was asking on the front page of that week's Observer.

The story was to have huge repercussions. Maidstone officials had read it and a copy was sent to the Lancaster Gate offices of the FA.

More stories followed, including one I was asked to write for the Daily Mail as it finally became clear that director Derek Southouse had sought the help of Bobby Drake's dad Ted in securing the services of a young Fulham youth keeper. He would play under the name of Micky Hayward. It was an away match so nobody would know…

Kevin Barry played in goal for the Tuesday night replay in which United played superbly to reach, or so they thought, the next round.

But the stories continued and the FA investigations were concluded. Their verdict: United would be thrown out of the prestigious Trophy tournament (which still has its final at Wembley) and fined £100.

The United board took their own action by fining Drake £80 and severely reprimanding director Southouse.

The editor's friendship with Bobby Drake came to an abrupt end and a week later I received a message via the editor, from Southouse, who acted in an unofficial press officer's role for United.

"Tell Ken McEwan he will never get another ounce of information out of me," was the message. Oh, dear.

A month later, I received a telephone call from Southouse.

"Ken, can we let bygones be bygones. I have just arranged a home friendly with Sheffield United and we need some publicity."

Of course we could. I had been doing my job as honestly as I could. It was time to move on. Our football clubs receive bags of publicity from the local press. We are not their press officers. We are answerable to the public – our readers – and nobody else. And whatever they may say, local clubs would not survive without the regular publicity from the local Press.

More recently, I ran into Southouse at an Eastbourne Borough match at Priory Lane. We both had a laugh as we recalled one of the dramatic episodes in United's history. It's true: time is certainly a great healer.

Cheating is something I have never been able to tolerate in sport. Winning fairly is surely what any game should be all about. Otherwise what satisfaction can be gained from success?

United had been proved well and truly guilty and some 30 years later the same could be said of two eminent professors at the University of Brighton, John Sugden and Gary Stidder.

Both men had deservedly received many accolades for their work in promoting peace overseas through the game of football, particularly in the Middle East,

Here in Eastbourne they jointly ran the Chelsea Academicals, a highly respected local side who won many honours at a humble level in the Eastbourne League.

On a Tuesday night at the Saffrons, I watched them beat the Q-Ball in the final of the Eastbourne Intermediate Cup, a popular local competition sponsored by the Herald.

I presented the trophy and medals to the Chelsea team after an exciting and entertaining match.

But a couple of months later the well-known sporting grapevine informed me that all was not well. In fact, it transpired that Chelsea had been forced to hand back the trophy to the Eastbourne FA after admitting fielding two ineligible players in the final.

There was no way it could be put down as an oversight. Two players, including a semi-professional goalkeeper, had been brought in at the 11th hour to strengthen the side.

When I spoke to the two professors, both referred me to the other, without actually admitting the misdemeanour. On the night of the final Stidder was receiving an award of his own at the Herald Achievers night, leaving Sugden in sole charge of the team.

It was an unhappy episode which seemed thoroughly out of character – Sugden had previously written a book called 'BadFellas' highlighting corruption in world football!

Our back page story took the local footballing community by great surprise and from what I understand, the two professors took quite a bit of stick within the corridors of power at the Eastbourne-based university campus.

My Sports Opinion piece, 'Black mark for the professors' did not pull any punches.

And Chelsea Academicals did not feature in the Eastbourne League the following 2008-09 season.

It is amazing how the most innocent of events can lead to the biggest stories and there was a further prime example that whether you are a player or an administrator, it doesn't pay to break the rules. This was another Sussex Intermediate Cup Final, between Eastbourne Town reserves and Shinewater AFC when yours truly again turned up to present the trophy at Priory Lane.

The match was progressing without controversy until late in the game when referee Dave Rogers sent off a Town player – the first of five dismissals (four Town and one Shinewater) for offences varying from fouls to abusive language.

Referee Rogers was a Polegate police constable, while his superior Detective Chief Inspector Kevin Moore was Town chairman. Afterwards Moore paid Rogers a visit in his dressing-room and allegedly let him know exactly what he thought about the red cards.

Rogers duly reported his superior to the Sussex FA for going uninvited into his dressing--room which Moore hotly denied. Inevitably all of this made headline stories on both front and back pages of that week's Eastbourne Herald.

Editor Peter Lindsey was quick to rush to the defence of a fellow ref and penned a damning front page editorial, highly critical of Moore under the headline 'Top Cops Collide.'

But Lindsey was a bit too quick in his criticism. Moore was later found not guilty by a Sussex FA Disciplinary commission and demanded a full apology in the Herald.

It was probably the best displayed apology ever to appear in the paper..

Whether it was warranted was another matter. Although Moore was let off by the FA, what could not be disputed was that he had been reported for misconduct after the game.

I turned up at the start of the evening game expecting to be home by 10.30pm. As it was I was still talking to ref Rogers after midnight.

9 Complications of a company car

IF a journalist was to give in his or her notice today, the most likely management reaction would be to find a cheaper replacement – if in fact a replacement was found at all. That is not necessarily a criticism of management but a stark reality in the economic climate in which we live.

But it was not always the case. Back in October, 1969 I was relaxing at home on a Friday night when the phone rang. It was Eric Redfern, who was about to take over as editor of the Eastbourne Gazette & Herald following the retirement of Bob Brutnell.

"How do you feel about becoming my sports editor?" Eric asked.

I had been at Hastings just over three years and loved the job. I was earning £25 a week with reasonable expenses. Eric offered me £32 a week with an extra £16 'guaranteed' expenses, double what I was getting already.

It sounded good to me and when I broke the news to a subdued Hastings editor John Cornelius who seemed to accept the inevitable – I was all but on my way to Eastbourne.

"FJ will never match that sort of money," he said. "It looks as if we'll have to give Elms a fat wage packet and let him get on with it."

I broke the news to worthy successor Philip Elms and he was delighted. It was the break he had been waiting for.

But a week later my 'departure' took a dramatic twist. Cornelius called me into his office. "McEwan, come in here," he beckoned in his so familiar gruff tone.

"About this Eastbourne offer, FJ wants to know if you would like a car. And we can put you up to Simpson's (news editor Ken Simpson's) rate. So you'll be on £28 a week."

The rise was fair, but the car was something else. Nobody but the editor was ever allocated a personalised company car. In those days it was a genuine perk, a brand new mini, tax free and all costs paid by the company – and I could sell my own car and put the money in the bank.

It was an offer I couldn't refuse. And when I bumped into FJ on the stairs a couple of days later I thanked him.

Cornelius was happy, I was delighted. But I had two things to do, firstly break the news to Eric Redfern. And then tell Phil Elms that his 'fat wage packet' would remain considerably thinner. Both had to wait 10 years virtually to the day before they got what they wanted.

In October, 1979, I finally became sports editor of the Eastbourne Gazette & Herald. And Phil took over the sports chair at Hastings which he was to occupy for the next 16 years.

There was one complication about having the luxury of a company car. I was to tell nobody, particularly those with whom I shared an office, Ken Simpson and Terry Fieldson, the joint news editors.

I felt uncomfortable with this situation until, some six months later, Simpson wanted a private word. My discomfort was eased when he said, "Don't worry, I know about the car, I'm getting one too."

That was fair enough, but it left Terry Fieldson, an Observer veteran who was working on past retirement age, out in the cold.

Fieldson was a good, honest man and a highly competent journalist with many years' service to the company, but not one of the editor's favourites. I really didn't like the fact that he was not being treated as we were, particularly as we were working so closely. But I had no option but to say nothing.

Then, one day, the secret was blown apart. Company secretary Ray Wild entered our office. All three of us were at our desks.

"No problems, I just want a few details about your cars," he called out at the door. First Simpson and then I furnished him with the relevant facts.

Ray Wild thanked us and made towards the door. "Hold on," yelled Fieldson. "You haven't got my details yet."

"I don't need them," replied Wild. "You haven't got a company car."

Needless to day, Fieldson blew his top. We had been close colleagues and good friends.

He understandably felt he had been betrayed. He started to pen a letter of protest to FJP, but didn't finish it. He was over the age of 65 and decided to keep his head down.

But I had the feeling he never looked on Simpson and myself in the same way again.

10 The battle with Derek's biscuits

REGULAR contact with local soccer managers is part and parcel of a sports editor's life. They are a mixed bunch. Always ready to speak to you when things are going well, less available when they have reached the stage of receiving that dreaded chairman's 'vote of confidence.'

Former Eastbourne United manager Gerry Boon, who sadly died in 2009 after a battle with cancer, was a favourite of mine. He would be open and honest about his team, his players and sometimes his committee.

A stern disciplinarian, he was renowned for getting the best out of youngsters, hence the famous 'Boon Babes' of the late '70s and early '80s.

When the diminutive Barry Winter was club chairman, six-foot plus Boon was his usual forthright self. "If I need anything, I just sit the chairman on my lap and tell him what I want," he once told me.

In one match report, I had been scathing in my criticism of young striker Derrick Smith, saying words to the effect that the speedy striker had appeared completely disinterested in what was going on in the game.

A couple of weeks later Boon beckoned me over. "I want to have a word with you about what you said about Derrick Smith," he said.

I feared the worst.

But surprise, surprise. Boon went on, "I just wanted to thank you. He was so wound up by what you said, he was man of the match last week. I didn't have to say anything; you did my job for me."

Dave Shearing was great fun and was always ready with a quick quip in reply to just about any question. His County League side Shinewater Association were going through a particularly bad time. "Would it be fair to say you have reached a crisis situation?" I asked.

"Crisis" replied Dave. "The only crisis we have at Shinewater is when the beer runs out."

Mick French was always honest in talking about his team's performance and, during his days in charge of Hailsham and United, was usually well prepared for his weekly phone call with a headline making quote.

Eastbourne Borough boss Garry Wilson has always been very good with the Press in that he was always readily available after matches, whether his side had enjoyed the best of wins or the heaviest of defeats.

Behind the dressing-room walls one could sometimes hear his Scottish accent effing and blinding at the players, only to appear before the Press with a wry smile and an ultra-professional summing-up of the game.

I remember criticising Ady Colwell for missing Town's first ever match in the Ryman League at Whitstable. Colwell was on a holiday break with his wife and I suggested his absence was tantamount to the vicar having a day off on a Sunday.

While I earned a text message of congratulations from former editor Peter Lindsey, the comment did not go down well with Town supporters.

There was never a dull moment when the former Eastbourne Town manager Trevor Wood was in charge at the Saffrons.

Wood was one of Town's most successful managers during the mid-80s but when they had not performed to his expectations he would say so in no uncertain manner.

"If only I could have had 11 substitutes I would have taken the lot off," he stormed to me after one game.

But maybe he had good reason to be critical. After knocking back a few beers at Town's annual dinner, Wood admitted to me that he had spent £1,000 out of his own pocket in player-payments during the season.

I was going straight off on holiday the next day so typed out what I felt was a really good story for the following week's paper. Alas it never appeared.

Wood had phoned a colleague on the Monday pleading that he had been drunk and 'please would we not print anything of what he may have said."

I am not sure I would have been so lenient in not using the story. If Wood had any inkling of what he said, he could not have been that drunk. And I have always believed that players' 'expenses' should not be a secret.

After all, we all have to pay income tax on anything we earn. Why should they be above the law?

Kenny McCreadie, who was in charge at Hailsham for five years, was rarely out of the headlines. A passionate Scot, it is probably fair to say he would not have been on any referee's Christmas card list.

He ended up in court for punching a United player after a local derby and he regularly gave refs a hard time at The Beaconsfield.

I criticised him on many an occasion in Sports Opinion, but McCreadie took it all in good heart.

"I am not the big, bad wolf you make me out to be," he once pleaded.

Although I would never condone attacking a player or swearing at the ref, McCreadie gave us many good stories.

Overall, I had an excellent relationship with local soccer managers. None more so than Sammy Donnelly, who had spells in the chair at Town and United in the early '80s and is currently in charge of the Sussex team.

Keeping the Press informed was high on the list of Donnelly's priorities, even to the extent of bringing his star signing Glen Geard into my office the moment he had secured the talented striker's signature. Geard, once on the books of Arsenal, had a shocking disciplinary record and Donnelly vowed to tame him. He succeeded and Geard went on to score many memorable goals at the Oval, reaching 50 in a single season.

Brian Dennis has been United's most successful manager since their merger with Shinewater and was always ready with a good quote. United AFC won the County League title in 2009. "I plonked a bottle of brandy on the table and told them to get some fire in their bellies" he once told his players during a half-time pep talk.

One man who was not a manager but who often acted like one was Derek York, formerly Eastbourne United treasurer and later secretary of Hailsham Town. Derek and I had a love-hate relationship and Derek probably featured in Sports Opinion more than any other person.

Ridiculous though it may seem, it was my regular criticism of his half-time refreshments that provided a major talking-point among the local fans.

Derek's biscuits (for home and visiting committees and the Press) were renowned as being hard and stale and I would regularly say so. "Derek's got his biscuits ready for you Ken" people would say to me when I turned up at The Beaconsfield.

"How are the teeth?" would be the second half question, with the first half of the actual game seemingly forgotten.

Sports Opinion could be serious, but it could also be fun. Sometimes it could be both.

Derek's infamous biscuits were always guaranteed to raise a smile, even though Derek himself was not always smiling.

Ken receives the congratulations of Eastbourne Borough legend Darren Baker at his retirement bash. Right: Ken and Kathy renew their marriage vows in St Lucia in 2009. Below: Taking sherry with World Cup winning captain Bobby Moore and his first wife Tina at a Hastings football dinner.

And the crowd go wild ... the Mighty Mac completes the Eastbourne 10-mile fun run. Right: Young Ken's first scoop - the story of a runaway horse. Below: Ken, standing second left, with the Argus football team whose good behaviour (one booking in 12 seasons) earned an appearance on Match of the Day.

Down the hatch ... party time in Majorca. Right: halfway to retirement as the pre-press boys offer a traditional tribute amid great hilarity. Below: The spectacular company Christmas party at the White Rock Pavilion, Hastings. Hokey-cokey Ken clings on to Bexhill colleague Beryl Parker while Mr and Mrs F. J. Parsons join in the fun.

11 My nightmare year

I ADMIT I was pretty fortunate during my journalistic career. While new technology and recessions resulted in many colleagues, mostly printers, falling by the wayside, I took very slightly early retirement just eight months short of the winning post.

There have been many challenges to meet, many obstacles to clear. But there was one year I would be more than happy to wipe off the calendar.

The year of 1979 began badly with much industrial unrest among printers at the Hastings Observer. The previous year had seen an all-out strike by the NGA (National Graphical Association). There had also been unrest among SOGAT (Society of Graphical and Allied Trades), the unskilled printers' union.

This had resulted in many weeks of banned overtime which usually meant, as deadline approached, my three broadsheet pages being reduced to two, resulting in many reports not seeing the light of day. There were also occasions when pages went through uncorrected, always a journalist's nightmare with what we always regard as 'literals' appearing in the paper.

The Easter of 1979 saw another SOGAT banning of overtime with the paper prepared and ready to roll on the presses. On the Thursday night I answered a call to help with the deliveries. I had many friends among SOGAT members, but the potential non-appearance of newspapers was putting livelihoods at stake.

It was an awful Thursday evening. I was given a huge van to deliver giant bundles of the Hastings and Bexhill Observers to newsagents in and around Hastings and Bexhill. I recall a moment of sheer panic as the van's sliding door stuck and would remain open with the road looking a very long way down as I drove apprehensively along thankfully deserted areas. There were no seat belts in those days and it was with huge relief when I made my final delivery at 3am on Good Friday and gratefully returned the van – the door remaining stuck – to base.

The management was delighted. MD Brian Nicklin took us out to dinner at the Beauport Park Hotel and a fun table tennis tournament followed a superb meal.

I assumed that was the end of the matter, but it was not. Seven months later, even though I had left the group, having moved to Eastbourne, I received a cheque for £250 through the post from the parent company, Westminster Press, expressing their gratitude that all the papers had reached their destinations on time. On today's values that cheque would be worth around double that amount..

The troubles of 1979, however, went from bad to worse. When the sports editor's position again became vacant at Eastbourne, I didn't hesitate. This time there was no FJ Parsons nor John Cornelius (who had been moved to Bexhill) around to offer me a better deal.

Now during his first decade as editor at Eastbourne Eric Redfern had a terrible reputation regarding the treatment of his staff. I had always got on extremely well with him, he having been a past chairman of the National Union of Journalists and me a past treasurer.

So I did not really believe the horror stories I had so often heard about life at Eastbourne. How wrong I was.

My move from Hastings to 18 miles along the coast was to reduce me to the lowest ebb of my life. One problem was that Eric had been editing the sports pages himself for at least three months prior to my arrival. His son Steve played for Eastbourne Town who were dominating the headlines.

On the other hand Eastbourne United, who were playing a higher standard of football in a superior league were being virtually ignored.

One of my first jobs was to redress the balance and somehow restore credibility to the sports pages – a job that was to prove easier said than done. From day one, I had people coming in and out of my office warning me about Eric. Soon I was to realise that the warnings were not without merit, but they were too late to save me.

At Hastings, I had enjoyed 13 years of total autonomy. When it came to the sports pages, my word was law, it was never questioned. On matters of finance of course I would consult the editor who was generally sympathetic to whatever cause I was needing cash for.

But when it came to the content and layout of the sports pages I was well and truly my own boss. That was not the case under Redfern who would insist on seeing all sports pictures before me.

An Eastbourne Town team picture had just been taken that weekend. It arrived on my desk with the instruction – use at least across five columns. Son Steve needed to be easily recognised!

Next the editor's secretary delivered to me a Town programme mentioning Steve Redfern had been chosen for Sussex. It was ringed with another instruction – story and pic for Herald MUST.

I wandered upstairs to meet the paper's four sub-editors. Reporters, most of them girls, were queuing outside the editor's office. I watched as one by one came out, most of them in tears. I suddenly realised – I had walked out of a dream job – and into a nightmare.

I didn't sleep that night – nor the following night. When I finally got to the weekend I had not slept a wink for six days.

That Saturday, I was covering Eastbourne Town at Little Common, the open recreation ground being a stark contrast to the warm, friendly Press box I had enjoyed at the Pilot Field, home of Hastings United. All I could think of was a burning desire to put back the clock, return to Hastings and work comfortably ever after.

Now when you have a bad or interrupted night's sleep, you feel pretty wretched the next day.

My second week at Eastbourne started with my mind totally disoriented after a week without sleep. It was like an emotional storm raging inside me.

I would normally have completed my Town report within an hour. This one had taken me most of Sunday to put together.

That second week at Eastbourne began in a daze. There were a couple more memos from the editor waiting on my desk, one suggesting I take a more in-depth look at park football, the other telling me to call a meeting of photographers for detailed guidance on improving football pictures.

It was all a case of Eric producing the bullets and me having to fire them. And it all did nothing to help my state of mind.

I started work on my first pages of the Gazette. I was sweating so decided to take a walk. I wasn't thinking logically. Absent-mindedly, I wandered across the road and was narrowly missed by a bus.

I certainly did not want my life to end, but my total despair at what I now considered a disastrous career move had taken over my mind.

Returning to the office, I decided to thrash things out with the editor. Never during my 13 years at Hastings had I received a memo saying what I should or should not do with my sports pages.

Needless to say, when I reached Eric's office he was involved in a row with another member of staff. In fury I started to make my way back downstairs.

These particular stairs had claimed several victims and I was merely the latest.

I must have lost my balance on the top stair. I lost consciousness and finally came round at the bottom with a concerned group around me waiting for the ambulance to arrive.

Somewhere in the background I could hear Eric recalling how he had been carted off to hospital with a heart attack a couple of years earlier. Now it was my turn, only in different circumstances. By the time we had reached hospital I was fully conscious, the main damage being a bruised head and broken glasses.

I was given a complete check over and discharged. I would have returned to the office, but the editor had given instructions that I should be driven home.

I was told to have a check-up with the doctor and was signed off work for two weeks. My depression did not improve despite sympathetic calls from colleagues and friends, including Phil Elms, Ken Simpson and David Gemmell, the then deputy editor of the Hastings Observer, who went on to become a best-selling author. Sadly, David Gemmell and Ken Simpson have since died.

Although I had left the company Hastings MD Brian Nicklin kindly sent round a psychiatrist. But that did not help. The only solution I wanted was to return to Hastings and that was not an option. The job was filled by Phil Elms, the person I had recommended for it.

John Cornelius was kind enough to offer me a sports editor's position on the Bexhill Observer and I also had the chance to work at East Grinstead. Both posts carried greatly reduced salaries to the one I was receiving at Eastbourne.

At home I must have been impossible to live with but Kathy was my rock with her devoted support and unbelievable patience. Without her I dread to think what would have been the outcome.

My mother-in-law would come round to ask Kathy how I was, with me just a few yards away apparently incapable of providing an answer.

After 10 terrible days at home I managed to reach a decision. I would return to Eastbourne on a short-term basis. My intention was to leave by Christmas.

Returning to my desk at Eastbourne was the hardest thing I have ever had to do. I found a parking place and sat in my car for 20 minutes. "I can't do it," I said to myself. "But I have to."

I received a very warm welcome back from my new Eastbourne colleagues. Despite my continual yearning to return to Hastings I felt I was among new friends. But Eric didn't make it easy for me in what I was to discover was very much a divide and rule reign.

The next Saturday Steve Redfern scored a rare goal for Town, a brilliant header in the opening minutes. The Sussex Express carried a superb action picture of it in their Friday edition. Sadly our photographer was five minutes late and missed it entirely.

When I showed Eric the sports page proofs that week, his reaction was exactly as I feared. He had watched the game and out came the inevitable question, "Why didn't our photographer get a picture of the first goal (he did not mention his son's name)?

"I think she was delayed in getting to the ground and was a few minutes late for the start," I replied.

As quick as a flash Eric was on the phone to the photographic department, asking to speak to the chief photographer, Annette Raffe (now Annette Perry).

"Mr McEwan wants to know why your photographer was late in getting to the Saffrons on Saturday which resulted in her missing a vital goal?" he demanded.

Needless to say, my name was mud with the photographers. But I did go down to them and explain the situation. "Typical Eric" was their reply.

Despite the interference of the editor, I found myself somehow coping with my new and strange life at Eastbourne. I was still waking up at 4 in the morning, but at least those totally sleepless nights had become a thing of the past.

I continued to suffer periods of depression, but one amazing week seemed to change my life for the better.

It started on Monday with the delivery of my promised new company car, a gleaming white Ford Escort, which the company must have been put on hold during those opening, uncertain weeks.

Tuesday saw the surprise arrival of the £250 cheque from Brian Nicklin for my 'delivery' work the previous Easter at Hastings.

But the end of the week produced the greatest news of all. Kathy was expecting our first baby (Kevin), a brother for my three adopted children, Roger, Angela and Richard.

My previous tears of despair turned into tears of joy. Life had to be worth living once again. I knew I had to stay at Eastbourne for the foreseeable future.

But never did I realise it would be for the next 29 years.

12 Two sides of an eccentric editor

BY the start of the New Year in 1980 I was gradually coming to terms with my new life at Eastbourne. And I had come to appreciate that the eccentric editor Eric had two sides to him.

Yes, he could be a pain in the proverbial backside. But he could also be kind and generous. His moods though were quick to change.

Just before Christmas I was working on the Gazette one night and he came into my office with a huge sack. It was full of toys, overspills from newspaper competitions. "Thought you might like them for the kids," he said. "I know they can't have too much at Christmas."

And in the week leading up to Christmas he would leave a bottle of whisky by the coffee machine to top up that much needed mid-morning drink – thankfully the drink-drive laws were not as strict in those days.

In my early months at Eastbourne I became increasingly indebted to sports reporter Steve Breach, who in the spring would become my first full-time deputy.

Steve had introduced me to many of the local sporting personalities and was an avid speedway follower, providing me with excellent reports of the Eastbourne Eagles' exploits.

In the afternoon of New Years' Day, Steve was due to report Eastbourne United's game at Lewes. He was also due into the newsroom at 9am for general news duties.

At 9.30am there were no sign of Steve. Eric was on the phone to me. "Have you seen Breach?"

"No," I replied.

"Well, if he can't be bothered to get here on time to do news, he needn't be bothered to do sport. You will have to take him off the United game. He can consider himself suspended."

The phone slammed down. Steve arrived at 9.45am obviously having enjoyed himself on New Year's Eve. I explained the situation to a bewildered Steve that he was free to return home – suspended.

However, this was one occasion when I was able to put one over Eric who went home at midday as it was January 1st.

I got on the phone to Steve, suggesting he still covered United, but I would not give him a byline. Steve agreed, wrote his report and reported for duty as usual the next morning.

Eric was none the wiser and never again mentioned the suspension.

I felt I was making progress on giving United their rightful share of publicity and it was a big occasion at The Oval when former England (and United) manager Ron Greenwood returned to his old stomping ground to switch on the Oval floodlights, before United beat Millwall 3-2 in a pulsating game,

The next day I joined United on a week's tour of Jersey and Guernsey, staying at an excellent hotel for which Eric had readily provided me with a company cheque.

Boon's Babes, as they had become known, gave an excellent account of themselves with skipper Dick Shepherd outstanding in central defence and players such as Mick Green in goal, Neil Ivemy and Russ Saunders in midfield and strikers John Kemp and Derrick Smith all giving outstanding performances.

But these were difficult days for Eastbourne Town who were suffering continual postponements at the Saffrons.

Rumours were rife that Saffrons chairman Alan Caffyn wanted the ground as the headquarters for Sussex Cricket Club. The days of senior football seemed to be numbered.

The County League were becoming increasingly disturbed at the number of postponements. On one occasion the referee arrived at the ground only to find it had been called off by secretary Dennis Shimmons due to waterlogging.

I spoke to the referee two days later and he was still steaming. "You could have held a wedding reception on that ground," he stormed.

I campaigned in the Herald to save football at the Saffrons, calling for MP Ian Gow, who was the Saffrons president, to get involved. Gow answered the call, attending a special Saturday morning meeting at the Saffrons. Soccer managed to survive, although footballers continued to be regarded as outsiders at the Saffrons.

More heady days arrived with the appointment of Roland Hutchinson as chairman and Trevor Wood as manager, although even when Town won the Sussex RUR Cup and challenged for the county league title the storm clouds refused to go away.

Hutchinson and Wood introduced payments to players. This was anathema to many of the Saffrons' old school including chairman David Stevens who was a great hockey man.

The Hutchinson / Wood reign was never going to last and calmer days behind the scenes did not arrive until the emergence of Roger Addems and Roger Cooper, both of whom had been Town managers.

These two, with the willing help of Angie Myall, did superb work behind the scenes to ensure football's survival and long-term stability.

Angie's husband Sid, the greatest Saffrons stalwart of all, had died of a heart attack during a game of table tennis. Sid had been a great player. He was voted the Athenian League's player of the year in Town's final season in that league.

He went on to become Town chairman and his death, along with that of legendary coach Taffy Jones, was a great loss to Town and the Saffrons.

But the two Rogers were men who lived and breathed the Saffrons. And when Roger Addems became chairman of both parent and football clubs, it meant that soccer at last had a major voice on the Saffrons committee.

Major ground improvements were masterminded. The most amazing was the installation of floodlights which had always met with huge residential disapproval from areas around the ground.

The arrival of lights heralded an upsurge in Town's fortunes and when the two Rogers decided to take more of a back seat, chairman Rupert Imich and manager Ady Colwell finally guided Town out of the County League and into Ryman Division One South.

How suddenly times can change. The end of 2009 saw the resignation of Colwell and in March 2010 the local soccer world was stunned when Imich died at the age of 47.

Slowly but surely I felt I was making progress with the sports pages and getting the balance of the United / Town coverage just about right. Eric was not complaining and must have been happy with my efforts when he named me Journalist of the Year in his annual Herald review. His comment that he regarded me as the best sports writer in Sussex was appreciated but typically Eric going over the top.

He again demonstrated a great act of generosity by nominating me as the official Beckett courier for a cruise of the Norwegian Fjords aboard the Canberra. I was summoned to the boardroom and given the official news by chief executive Derrick Platt.

It was to leave on Friday, June 13 for 14 nights and even the fact that I had my annual holiday already booked did not seem to matter. It simply meant that during the month of June that year I spent just four days in the office.

As an added bonus there were two coachloads of Beckett passengers from East and West Sussex which meant that Kathy could accompany me free of charge. It was a marvellous moment as we set sail from Southampton and when we reached our cabin another surprise – a huge bouquet of flowers wishing us bon voyage – signed by Eric Redfern.

But while 1986 was a good year for me, it saw the demise of Eric. The first phase of new technology had arrived and Derrick

Platt had introduced his eventual successor as chief executive Kevan Regan who initially joined the company as general manager.

We were all aware of goings-on in the background and it was finally announced that Eric would be taking early retirement – seven years early. Eric made it clear that he was not happy with the situation but in the eyes of the big bosses the exit door appeared to be his only option.

He retired at the end of 1986 and was succeeded by Hugh Rowlings. Eric subsequently joined the local freesheet, the Eastbourne News, which was then edited by Sally Wellings, a former Gazette reporter and Sussex Express editor.

As I had for the previous six years, I continued to give Eric a lift to Eastbourne Town away games and it was easy to detect his despair at losing the power he had enjoyed for some 17 years. He had become a keen golfer at the Eastbourne Downs Golf Club and it was on the golf course where he was to suffer a heart attack. He died a week later before he was 60.

The letter pages of the Gazette & Herald were filled with tributes and rightly so. Under his editorship, the papers had flourished. The news pages were busy and controversial and Eric's weekly political column was feared by councillors of all political colours. People everywhere moaned about Eric but they never stopped buying his papers.

We had all suffered under Eric, and he had virtually driven me to a nervous breakdown when I joined the paper. But in many ways he made us stronger. After somehow surviving seven years under his editorial leadership, I felt fit to survive anything and anybody. Others who complained about future editors would not have survived Eric.

He was the absolute Jekyll and Hyde and is still talked about today among journalists who served under him more than 20 years ago. We shall certainly not see his like again.

13 Ecstasy – and agony

I HAVE always believed that sports editors and sports writers should have some experience of playing the game they are reporting on. It's easy to criticise. But when you have been there yourself you should have more understanding of any given situation.

My sporting career – albeit on a modest level – was often a rollercoaster ride with moments of ecstasy and agony, highs and lows which every sportsman enjoys and suffers.

Soccer was always my number one sport from the day I made my debut in the West St Leonards Primary School team. I was actually told off by our football teacher for passing the 11+ a year early at the age of 10 – he was planning to make me the school soccer captain the following season.

From day one at the Hastings Grammar School I was anxious to impress on the soccer field. And it was on day one that my progress was to come to a temporary halt due to a personal act of crass stupidity.

We were having a kickabout at the end of the school day and it developed into an unofficial game of six-a-side. Among the opposition was a player who genuinely annoyed me. I had known him at West St Leonards and he had moved on with me to the grammar school. His name was Andrew Hersey and he would walk around with a smirk on his face as if he was taking the mickey out of anyone and everyone.

I decided to wipe the smirk off his face. He had the ball and I went into him – hard. It was never intended to be a career-threatening challenge, just a lot harder than I would normally tackle. We both fell to the ground and I remained there in agony, my wrist broken, while he got up wearing that same irritating smirk.

Never had I been so annoyed with myself. The first day at a new school, sports masters on the lookout out for a future

Stanley Matthews and I was in hospital having my arm put in plaster - and it was entirely my own fault.

After three weeks I could stand no more. I pleaded to be included in a house soccer trial and was allowed to play. And I managed to score a goal – with my arm in plaster.

I went on to establish myself in the school teams from under-12 to 15 and was vice-captain of the under-15s in my final year.

I joined Hastings Rangers at the age of 15, but a year later was persuaded to move to Bexhill Town by Tony Tubb, my new work colleague on the Bexhill Observer and a regular member of the senior side. I was fortunate enough to score twice on my debut for Bexhill reserves, but really enjoyed my games in the Bexhill youth team along with another great friend, Barry Salvage, who was later to enjoy a wonderful professional career in England and America before losing his life in the 1986 Eastbourne Fun Run.

During his days with Fulham, I watched Barry in action against Manchester United for whom George Best was playing. Barry went on to play professionally in America and to manage in Norway. He finally returned to Sussex and had just opened a sports shop in Eastbourne.

Short of training, he had made a last-minute decision to enter the fun run and collapsed and died about 100 yards before the finish. What a sad day that turned out to be.

Barry and I struck up a great strike partnership and we were both given games in the Bexhill Town senior team in the County League division one before Barry was spotted by Gordon Jago and whisked off to Eastbourne United.

Barry actually bought my first motor-scooter, paying off the money at £5 a month. We were to laugh about that in later years when Barry was on mega-bucks as a professional footballer and manager.

My playing career reached a temporary halt when I moved to the Tonbridge Free Press, but it came alive again on my return to Hastings as sports editor of the Hastings Observer.

Although I was covering football on Saturdays, an Evening Argus Sunday team had been entered in the Hastings Sunday League and I was invited to join.

This time I was to benefit from the skills of Tony Tubb who operated like a wizard on the left flank, making numerous goals for me. There was one game I will never forget. I woke up early Sunday morning feeling ill after a party the night before. In fact I was too ill to get to the phone to let manager Alan Barton know I would be unable to turn out.

As it got towards 10am I decided to struggle to the Bexhill Downs (our home ground) in the hope there would be an extra player available who would be able to take my place. Needless to say there was nobody and Alan persuaded me to at least start the game and come off if I wasn't feeling up to it.

I agreed and within five minutes had scored the opening goal. I immediately felt better and found the net again … and again … and again … In fact, I ended up with nine goals in the 13-2 win against King's Arms which at that time was a Sunday League record. I felt immensely proud to see a panel recording the fact on the back page of the next day's Evening Argus, headed Good Old Ken.

The following Sunday we faced the Fishermen's team who were renowned as one of the most physical in the league. The Whites are one of the best known soccer families in Hastings and marking me was Conky White a rough, tough centre-half. "Nine-goal McEwan" he sneered before the game, "You won't be scoring nine goals today."

Conky gave me a torrid time and even rugby tackled me when I was clean through on goal. A timid young referee seemed too scared to give me any protection and Conky got away with murder. A far more experienced referee by the name of Derek Graham who was watching the match said afterwards he would have sent Conky off in the second half. That didn't help me and we ended up losing 4-2.

Our Argus team did not win many trophies. But we did play to the rules and we didn't whinge to referees.

Imagine our delight then, when our team picture appeared on BBC's Match of the Day. We were featured as an example to the professional game which at that time was being ruined by players being sent off or booked. We had played through 12 seasons with just a single yellow card.

My competitive playing days – or so I thought – ended when I joined the Eastbourne Gazette & Herald in 1979. I still took part in the odd five-a-side tournament and was privileged to be included in the Eastbourne United Veterans lineup against Arsenal Celebs in 2006. More than 1,000 people flocked to the Oval to see the likes of Groundforce presenter Tommy Walsh and former world champion boxer Terry Marsh. Although we were beaten 7-1 I thoroughly enjoyed the experience and there was actually a queue for my autograph afterwards! Who did they think I was?

It was a great experience to be included in a veteran Hastings Observer team that played the BBC at Bisham Abbey, the national sports centre of excellence. We were well beaten by the BBC whose side included long-serving soccer commentator John Motson.

I went on to score a hat-trick for United Vets in an Eastbourne League six-a-side game before my career abruptly came to a close at the ripe old age of 63.

The Gazette & Herald's six-a-side charity tournament at the Saffrons had become an established part of Eastbourne's sporting calendar and I was delighted to be a member of the Gazette team. We all agreed to take a turn in goal in the absence of an established keeper and when my turn came I was thoroughly enjoying it even surprising myself with a couple of decent saves.

Then a high ball was lobbed into the area about 10 yards out. I have always believed that good keepers should have a command of their goal area and I dashed out to punch the ball clear, getting there momentarily before the head of Eastbourne United's Lee Walsh. At precisely the same time my deputy sports editor Derren Howard careered in like a tank to head clear.

The three of us collided and I found myself laid out on the ground unable to move, virtually unable to breathe. After a few minutes I was able to struggle to my feet, a few broken ribs restricting my movement.

For a week, I was virtually unable to move my neck. Changing gear in my car was agony. Slowly the pain eased until a month later in a pool in Barbados I found I was unable to swim, just the effort of turning my arm over giving me excruciating agony. With the aid of Kathy, I started to learn breaststroke, but to onlookers in the pool it must have looked as if I was recovering from a stroke.

It was several months before I was clear of the pain. Somebody suggested that Derren had been seeking early promotion, but that was (I think) just a joke.

However, it was no joke recovering from one of my most painful experiences and I decided there and then. My footballing days were over after more than half a century in the thick of the action.

I was never a great cricketer although I turned out regularly for the Observer and Gazette cricket teams.

I was a very poor man's Geoffrey Boycott, opening the batting but painfully slow at scoring runs. My team-mates, acknowledging my limitations, would reassure me that I was a valuable asset in seeing off the fast bowlers. I usually got out when the slow men were brought on and they could reap the resultant run harvest.

In one match against Ore I was at my most painful, batting unchanged throughout the innings with a final score of nine. I did have my moments and actually reached 48 on one occasion, but I always reckoned that my fielding was of most benefit to my team. I rarely dropped a catch and some of the catches that I held would have been regarded as impossible by others.

I generally kept clear of injuries until, during one game, I was playing for the Observer against Beaulieu.

The ball had been dispatched to the boundary and when a fielder threw it back I helped it on its way towards the bowler. But in doing so I dislocated my thumb. It was agony and I could see myself taking no further part in the game – until a masterly stroke by one of our opponents who ran over and clicked my thumb back into place. What a great man!

I am afraid that I adopted the same, dour defensive outlook when it came to table tennis. Not that I had any intentions of taking up the game seriously. But when my son Kevin wanted to join the Westfield club at the age of 12 I was roped into his three-man team – largely because I was the only one able to provide regular transport.

And so I made my debut in the Hastings Table Tennis League at the age of 48.

Now Kevin was a natural and soon developed a range of classic attacking shots that would leave opponents in despair. I would give him plenty of practice on our table in the garden, him with his frighteningly fierce shots, backhand and forehand, me doing my best to return them.

Although I was a long way from being the gifted player Kevin was, I did develop an uncanny knack of returning even the hardest shot. I took this talent into the league and started to frustrate even the best of players.

In one game I watched in awe as a Welsh schoolmaster demoralised an opponent with an awesome display of table tennis. I dreaded playing him, thinking that I, too, would be the next for a thrashing.

But somehow, I managed to get back the best he could offer, frustrating him to such an extent that he would either smash the ball into the net or off the table. Suddenly, he lost the plot entirely, throwing his bat to the other end of the room.

Afterwards he apologised. "I have never done that in 30 years of playing league table tennis," he told me. "But in those 30 years you are the most awkward sod I have ever faced."

A combination of Kevin's flair and my defence took us up the divisions from six to two. And it was a proud moment when, in the summer of 1996 we won the Hastings League handicap tournament with me getting a maximum in the final. On the way to the final we (Hastings Tigers) had an amazing match against Saints, losing the first four matches out of nine. Trevor Towner had played his three and said a sad goodbye thinking we were on the way out of the tournament. But we won the next five to reach the final.

We also played in the Eastbourne League, our Central club winning the division three title. I went 54 games unbeaten and was informed by the late John Woodford, for many years the Gazette & Herald table tennis correspondent, that this was a league record.

And so to road running. When Eric Redfern came into my office to ask what I thought of the paper organising a marathon open to runners of all ages and abilities, I said it was a good idea, but the hours needed for the organisation of such an event would be enormous. Little did I realise that at that moment the seeds of what was to become one of Eastbourne's largest ever sporting participant events were being planted. A year later the Eastbourne 10-Mile Fun Run was born.

Fortunately, the borough council took over the brunt of the organisation and the event caught the imagination of the public big-time. As sports editor I told Eric I would be happy to take part and it was an emotional experience being among 1,600 runners, of all ages and abilities, setting off up Lottbridge Drove with the tones of Chariots of Fire ringing in our ears.

Although I was always pretty nippy at short bursts, long distances were never my forte. I had done a bit a training but not nearly enough. At the five-mile mark I had maintained a reasonable pace, but during the second half of the run I began to wilt.

Instead of swallowing the welcome supply of water available at each mile post, I just threw it over my head as I sweated buckets. But the support from people at the roadsides was magnificent. Throughout the streets there was applause which certainly gave me renewed strength as I made my way along what seemed an everlasting last three miles on the seafront.

The Herald's golf correspondent of the day Charles Welsh threw me a mini bottle of whisky, so well meaning but unfortunately misguided. I saved it for the finish. There was amazing camaraderie among the contestants, particularly the strugglers such as myself. Talk about life beginning at 40 ….

It was a great feeling as I reached the finish. With two of my safety pins on my running vest having slipped I held my number in place so that my 80-minute time could be correctly recorded. A couple of ambulancemen thought I was holding my chest and about to have a heart attack and rushed over to administer first aid. But no, I only needed time to recover.

My wife Kathy, sister Joan and the children were in the distance. Son Kevin, aged five, rushed to meet me. "You've made it at last," he yelled. "I thought you had died". And then, after a moment's hesitation he added, "I'm glad you didn't."

In all I completed 10 Eastbourne fun runs, my time slowly worsening year by year until it finally reached the 100-minute mark. In later years I was joined by sons Richard and Kevin, daughter Angela and niece Annette.

When my two sons had to wait at the end for me to come in it was time to call it a day. But wonderful memories of a great event will always remain with me.

14 Terrifying technology

NEWS that modern technology was on the way did not enthral me. Truth to tell I was terrified of it. Whenever I visited schools to give a talk I was always impressed by the confident manner in which pupils coped with the computer age. Even more so when a certain teacher called for a nine-year-old to help her fix the print machine. She hadn't a clue!

But I grew up with none of that. The Three Rs were everything in my early schooldays – reading, writing and arithmetic – and they were never a problem for me. But computers? I kept well clear of them.

The first taste had come in 1986 when we were introduced to the tandy, a machine I regarded as my mobile typewriter which enabled me to write up football reports at home. This was a new ball game but one I was quickly able to master.

Five years later, when it came to producing entire pages electronically, that was something else. We went to Worthing to see a demonstration. It looked amazing but frightening. Menus had always been something I had enjoying browsing through in a restaurant. As for a mouse, I would simply call the cat! However they were now technology terms to which I was going to have to get very familiar in years to come.

It was in the early 90s when new technology hit us full in the face with the introduction of electronic pages.

A computer was delivered to the newsroom available for practice sessions prior to the real thing. Editor Hugh Rowlings was a technology wizard and one by one gave as an introductory session. After half an hour he left me to practise alone. Practise? I could barely control the mouse. I was hopeless.

At least a year elapsed before we were due to go live. Before then we were to have a week's official training.

In the meantime the odd page was being produced electronically. Another to take to new technology like a duck to water was my deputy at the time, Charles Goodall. It was his weekly duty to lay out the one sports page in the Eastbourne Advertiser and when he produced one on what I called the 'dreaded machine' I was full of admiration – and just a little jealous.

As the training week drew closer Charles could sense my apprehension and offered to give up half his regular day off to give me one-to-one weekly training sessions. I was deeply grateful even though, for the first time, I was in the slightly embarrassing position of learning from my deputy.

Very slowly and fairly surely the penny dropped and when official training began under a very intolerant girl in her mid-20s, I was just about able to keep up with the rest. Our trainer, however, was a disgrace, dismissing those of us with what she obviously regarded as silly questions with a scornful "I won't be here next week to save you."

Editorial trainer Carol Davies, who was even more of a novice than me when it came to computers, actually had to ask me for help because she dared not ask the trainer. Amazingly, I was able to assist her, but so grateful was I that I had mastered the basics thanks to the expertise of Charles Goodall.

The first week of producing our pages electronically live was a big test for all of us. But we seemed to get through.

I really thought I had arrived and there was nothing more to conquer. But sadly nothing quite works like that. Rumours were gathering of a big system change and once again I knew I would be struggling. But once again the gods were looking down upon me.

We had reached the year 2002 and Mark Dunford was my deputy and thankfully, he was another computer ace. I lost him for a month when he was chosen first to learn the new system and then give training sessions at Hastings and Eastbourne to the relevant sub-editors. After a couple of sessions I managed to get the hang of it with the benefit of having Mark close at hand when it went live.

Test number three came with a new picture system and the introduction of mediagrid. With Mark having been promoted to deputy editor at Crawley, it was chief sub Julia Northcott's turn to put us through our paces which she did pretty well. And what a marvellous system mediagrid is - with pictures available for use years after they have been processed.

How times have changed. When I arrived at the Pevensey Road offices of the Gazette & Herald in October 1979 it was the last week of the historic system with stories tapped out on typewriters ready to set them in hot metal before the pages were made up by compositors. There were just four sports pages in those days, two in the Gazette and two in the Herald.

When I left in February, 2009, deputy Derren Howard and myself were producing electronically a regular 14 pages a week (including 'specials' for the Hailsham and Seaford Gazettes). Remnants from the old days are many vacant desks once occupied by type-setters, make-up artists and pre-press workers.

Both at Hastings and Eastbourne I enjoyed the banter with the printers on make-up days. They would follow our layout plans as best they could and sometimes we would either over or under-estimate the size of the stories. They loved it when there was a problem that was the fault of editorial and sometimes a few harsh words were exchanged, especially when deadline closed in. But it usually ended in good humour and there was many a time when I was grateful to the make-up man for his expertise – or even pointing out an error as most of them read the sports pages avidly.

Mick Grimer was an overseer at Eastbourne as well as being, for a spell, chairman of Langney Sports Football Club. At the time I was writing weekly leaders as it was one of my duties as assistant editor during the regime of Hugh Rowlings.

Langney Sports were going through a terrible time with players constantly being red carded for unbelievably bad discipline on the football field. I criticised them in a leader, suggesting Grimer was not doing enough to curb the bad discipline and that he should be weeding out the offenders and kicking them out of the club.

Grimer took exception and wanted that section of the leader omitted. I told him that if this happened it would be an abuse of his position. After all, none of the other clubs had chairmen working in the building and would only see the paper when it appeared in the newsagents. He got the same answer from editor Rowlings and ruefully accepted the situation. But a year or so on I got the impression that he was quite proud to have been mentioned in a Herald leader.

A similar situation did occur a couple of years later, however, involving Roly Hutchinson whose sudden death in the New Year was a great shock to us all. Roly was a great friend and in charge of the print-room. He also took on the mantle of Eastbourne Town chairman as well as being a local magistrate.

During a Town game at Horsham, there were one or two nasty fouls committed by the home men on Eastbourne players. "What do you feed them on, raw meat?" bellowed Hutchinson. "They need locking up."

I didn't consider this appropriate behaviour for either a visiting club chairman or a local magistrate and said so in Sports Opinion. Hutchinson saw it in advance and persuaded acting editor Steve Turner to take it out as he thought his action would lose him his status as a magistrate.

I was furious and when editor Hugh Rowlings returned from holiday, I got him to put it back in. He did – and Roly Hutchinson survived as a magistrate. But at least the freedom of the Press was upheld!

15 Newspapers publish them, doctors bury them

AS journalists we have always hated them. But sadly, they have always and will always happen. I am talking about errors. 'Newspapers publish them, doctors bury them' goes the saying. It's true, but no less painful.

I would be less than honest if I said I had not made my fair share of mistakes. And if I am aware of an error I have personally made on any page, I simply don't want to look at that page again.

There are two categories of errors, factual and literals. In the old days we usually managed to get ourselves off the hook by referring to them as 'printer's errors.' After all, no journalist could possibly be responsible for such stupidity … or could they?

Alas, we can no longer blame the poor old printer, simply because he does not exist.

From A to Z it is the journalist who is responsible for each piece of editorial on any given page. We can no longer hide behind the 'inefficient inkie.'

One of the most infamous errors to appear in the Hastings Observer actually appeared in the days of proof readers, who have sadly long been discarded .

It was an innocent enough story, the retirement of a popular primary school headmistress. As the report said, she would be missed by her many pupils – what a shame that in the word missed, the letter *p* had somehow replaced the letter *m*!

Then there was that well meaning organisation, the Royal Society for the Protection of Birds whose members were not amused when, in the paper, it appeared as the Royal Society for the *Prevention* of Birds.

The letters page is always a popular read, but the unfortunate omission of just one letter did not bring a smile to one mourning widower as he recalled with great feeling those happy years he had been married to a 'fine American lay'. Oh dear, whatever happened to the *d* in that final word?

Of course, not every error is the responsibility of editorial. Things have also been known to go wrong in the advertising department.

A well-known local butcher paid a considerable sum of money to launch the opening of his new shop, boasting that his steaks would be 'hard to beat' - again that single letter *b* failing to appear.

And there was no consolation for a grieving family when, in the deaths column they had to read of the passing of 'a very dead dad.' They did, of course, mean a *dear* dad, but once the paper is printed, there is no way back, no matter how embarrassing the error.

Of course, there have also been mistakes that fortunately didn't get in, those spotted at the 11th hour by a last-gasp eagle eye.

The most notable was so nearly committed by former Eastbourne Herald editor Peter Lindsey. There had been various ceremonies across Eastbourne following the death of Princess Margaret. Right on deadline Peter found he had an empty page to be filled with pictures / stories of Princess Margaret tributes.

When he had completed the page he asked my deputy Mark Dunford to 'send' it to Portsmouth where all our newspapers are now printed. Mark was about to press the final button when he noticed something wrong with the headline. In big, bold type, it said, 'Town says farewell to Princess Royal.' That so nearly became a classic error, the Princess Royal, of course, being Princess Anne.

Peter's sigh of relief echoed round the town.

16 My clash with Ian Gow

HUGH Rowlings' arrival as group editor of the Eastbourne Gazette & Herald in succession to Eric Redfern seemed to bring a wave of sanity around the offices in Commercial Road.

Hugh was very much a hands-on editor and a master of new technology When he took over in January, 1987, with his wife Julia joining the sub-editorial team, local newspapers were booming. A boardroom celebration was held to celebrate the first 100-page Herald. Derrick Platt was in his final months as chief executive and he was to be succeeded by Kevan Regan.

Rowlings made no secret of the fact that he liked the look of the Gazette & Herald sports pages and one of his first acts was to promote me to the position of assistant editor, number three in the pecking order under himself and deputy editor Steve Turner.

I had mixed feelings about the promotion. It meant saying goodbye to sport, taking on the responsibility for the company's special productions such as the Holiday Times, editing the then booming free paper, the Eastbourne Advertiser, and filling in on the subs' desk when any of the regular subs' team was away.

The position also required me to become the leader writer for the Herald and the three Gazettes (Eastbourne, Hailsham and Seaford).

For all Eric's faults he wrote a brilliant comment, touching many a political nerve to the extent that most local councillors would shudder at the prospect of reading his latest attack.

So I had a hard act to follow, but I must have done it reasonably well for even when I returned to the sports desk 18 months later, I continued to write the leaders throughout Rowlings' 10-year reign as editor.

As in Sports Opinion, there are times when there is the need to criticise individuals, to the delight of many – but to the often obvious fury of the individual in the firing line.

I had always enjoyed an excellent relationship with Eastbourne's MP Ian Gow, who was so tragically murdered by the Provisional IRA in 1990.

I felt that regardless of his political colour, Gow did a superb job, always doing his best to look after the interests of his constituents.

When I had reason to criticise Gow, I could not help recalling yet again the wise words of LJ Bartley: "A good journalist when he retires has few friends, because if he has done his job properly he would have upset just about all of them at some time or the other."

It was General Election campaigning time when I upset Gow big time. An election hustings was planned at which all local candidates would be present at the same time facing questions from the floor. It seemed an ideal opportunity for voters to compare the views of each candidate on many of the big local and national issues.

However, Gow refused to attend, preferring to meet his constituents individually and at meetings at which he was the sole speaker. I was critical of his stance and when I felt he should have been at the all-party meeting I heard he was seen having a leisurely lunch..

I did not mince my words in that week's Herald leader. His rightful place was with the other candidates brave enough to face the firing line of the public at large.

Gow was furious, on the phone to me on publication day at 9am, accusing me in no uncertain terms of 'falling below your usual immaculate standards'.

He argued that his 'leisurely lunch' had consisted of a ham sandwich and a rushed pint of beer, finally slamming the phone down.

I reckoned it would be my last conversation with Gow. I was wrong. A few months later I had just completed the Eastbourne 10-mile run and suddenly saw the former housing minister making his way towards me. I envisaged another row or a sarcastic comment.

How wrong I was. 'Ken, you were magnificent,' he beamed and shook me warmly by the hand.

That, sadly, was my final encounter with the great man.

On July 30, 1990, Gow was murdered by the Provisional IRA when a bomb exploded as he started his car at his home at The Dog House in the village of Hankham.

It was a house that held many pleasant memories for me. Each Christmas and after every election campaign, Gow would invite the editorial staff of the Herald for a delightful buffet meal hosted by himself and his wife Jane who later became a Dame.

More than 3,000 people attended his funeral at St Peter and St Saviour's Church in Eastbourne.

His death had not only saddened his constituents, but had sent shock waves across the country. A personal friend of the then Prime Minister Margaret Thatcher, Ian Gow was, without doubt, Eastbourne's most popular MP.

As they would say in Yorkshire, he called a spade a spade. But he bore no grudges as I realised after that fine gesture at the end of the fun run.

During my 19 months on general news, I was receiving more money for working fewer hours. Several times I was in personal charge of the Gazette & Herald when Rowlings or Steve Turner were away.

I was also deeply involved in a special production recording the Great Storm of 1987 when Rowlings, Turner and myself edited page after page of dramatic pictures and stories depicting the catastrophic damage caused by winds of hurricane force.

On the day when I should have been celebrating my 43rd birthday, I was marooned in the office surrounded by storm stories and pictures.

The real hero of that event was picture editor Terry Connolly who battled through the night at great personal risk to himself to provide the Gazette & Herald and the subsequent supplement with graphic and dramatic pictures of an event that will never be forgotten.

But I missed the autonomy of the sports department and the sporting scene in general. I loved running my own show and it was just not the same on general news where the captain was always very much the editor.

So when my successor Rupert Taylor, moved on and Rowlings ask if I had any suggestions for the position of sports editor, I replied: "Yes, me."

Rowlings was surprised but agreeable and in July, 1988 I returned to the sports desk chair but continued to write the Gazette & Herald leaders. By doing this I retained my assistant editor status.

Being sports editor under Rowlings was as it should be. No interference and the sheer joy of being left to get on with the job.

Because of the midweek Gazette, life was always going to be harder than at Hastings, but at least I was my own boss again.

It was not, however, to last for ever. Huge changes began to take place within the Beckett empire.

Publishing giants Johnston Press bought out the Beckett group with uncomfortable repercussions for certain of the hierarchy. Out went Kevan Regan after five years as chief executive. Out went production director John Woodford.

In came Mike Pakes as the new MD. And off went Hugh Rowlings to edit the Sussex Express & County Herald. A new era was about to start with a young man named Peter Lindsey at the editorial helm.

17 From Langney Sports to Eastbourne Borough

DURING nearly 30 years at Eastbourne there was no greater story than the phenomenal rise of Langney Sports. I well remember the opening of the superb Langney clubhouse by Ian Gow MP and a conversation with a very young-looking chairman Len Smith.

"Come and join us for a drink any time. You don't have to be working. Just come and have a drink and relax," he said.

I have remembered those words over many years for the simple reason they have epitomised the friendliness with which Langney Sports and now Eastbourne Borough have always extended to me.

Over three decades Langney Sports / Eastbourne Borough have embarked on an amazing journey. From the humble surrounds of park football, on to intermediate status, through three divisions of the county league, into the upper regions of the Dr Martens eastern division, the Southern League premier, Nationwide South and now, unbelievably, the top tier of non-league football, the Blue Square Premier.

Inevitably, players have come and gone and so have managers. But Len Smith has remained at the helm along with Mick Grimer and the majority of his uniquely loyal committee. And despite moving into the heady heights of non-league football, Len and his committee have never changed.

True, there has been lively banter and even one or two crossed swords. But throughout all those years that warm welcome has never faltered despite the occasional murmur from vice-chairman Grimer that my free annual club dinner tickets might be in jeopardy.

Langney's progress up the non-league ladder has been well documented. Let's feature a few of the characters who contributed so immensely to the club's success.

Mick Green immediately comes to mind. The player whose career was so tragically cut short by death in a trench accident at work at the so early age of 32 was not just a gifted midfielder who was uniquely selected for Sussex both as a goalkeeper and outfield player.

He was a lovable rogue who was always ready to buy you a drink after the game – usually with a borrowed tenner. Mick had a great rapport with refs (although he was not on many of their Christmas card lists), the crowd – and the Press.

I can well remember when Mick had a rare off-day and I described his midfield position as appearing to be occupied by the Invisible Man. He was, however, back to his best the following week and during the game he spotted me as he was about to take a throw-in somewhere near the half-way line.

'You crucified me today,' he bellowed (the Herald in those days came out on a Saturday). 'But I'll forgive you if you make me MoM next week."

Pete Cherry was a manager who took Sports through all three divisions of the county league. He became a managerial legend at Priory Lane for 13 super years.

At each annual dinner Cherry would take the micky out of the first team squad by presenting each player with a suitable gift illustrating an unfortunate moment (or more) from the previous season.

On one such occasion there was a gift for me. Over the Easter holiday games I had credited a goal scored by Pete Roberts to Paul Callingham (the two players looked identical from a distance).

I had taken a lot of stick over the telephone from Pete Roberts' sister who told me I had spoilt her entire Easter – after all, brother Pete didn't score that many goals.

My gift from Cherry was a giant pair of glasses to help me see the players better and a large bottle marked 'poison' purporting to come from Roberts' sister.

On another occasion there was lively banter going on between Cherry and the then Hailsham boss Steve Richardson.

Following an incident on the field, Cherry went across and punched Richardson fairly and squarely on the nose. Richardson didn't respond. I wondered whether I had been seeing things.

I questioned Cherry about it later in the week, expecting a denial. On the contrary, he freely admitted it. 'So why did you do it?' I asked him. 'I hate the bloke,' was Cherry's reply.

There were many laughs over those 13 years and not too many denials when I hinted in Sports Opinion that most of the players did their training over the pool table.

When Sports won the third division of the county league the man guarding the Langney goal was a heavyweight by the name of Steve Dell.

County League chairman Peter Bentley (another one who seems to go on forever) forecast that Sports' progress into the higher echelons would result in Dell's demise.

Others uttered similar sentiments, but how wrong they all were. Big Steve may not have lost much in the way of weight, but he did gain more and more respect as he continued to keep goal admirably, playing a full part in Sports' division one success.

He certainly deserved his testimonial match against Brighton and Hove Albion in the days when David Bellotti was Albion's chief executive and a regular visitor to Priory Lane.

Sports have had many gifted players over the years. One was striker Nigel Hole whose unbelievable control over the ball would enable him to create a chance out of nothing – his two amazing strikes against Littlehampton taking Sports into the Sussex Senior Cup Final for the first time were typical examples.

Sadly, Hole's career was also cut short by a badly broken leg sustained in the Stamco goalmouth during an early-season match in the 90s.

Hole did attempt a comeback but was never quite the same again, lacking that burst of speed so vital in his executions.

What have been my greatest memories during my sports-watching years? Obviously there have been many. The three pulsating FA Cup ties against Kingstonian (92-93), which ended in defeat for Sports after Kingstonian had won the toss for home advantage in the third game must rank highly.

And for sheer drama there was little to beat the FA Cup shoot-out against Berkhamsted or that never-to-be forgotten night at Leylands Park (Tuesday, April 11, 2000) when Sports beat Burgess Hill to make their great escape from the county league.

Celebrations were in real style after the final whistle with manager Garry Wilson and assistant Nick Greenwood joining the players in diving into the thick goalmouth mud.

Mark Goodwin coming on to score the goal that won the senior cup for the first time will live in the memory forever and two seasons ago, there were many tense and thrilling moments as promotion was gained into the Blue Square Premier.

People sometimes ask about the greatest goal ever scored at Priory Lane and that is a tough one. Nigel Hole, Simon Kibler, Scott Ramsay, Paul Armstrong, Matt Crabb and Andy Atkin have all made some amazing strikes.

But my vote would go to a scorer who, as a player, would not feature on anyone's list of all-time local greats. Jeremy Creed was tall, tense and awkward. Pull the ball back to him six yards out of goal and he would often fall over it.

Yet in the FA Cup against Harrow Borough, he put away one of the most amazing strikes I have ever seen. Picking up the ball inside his own half, Creed seemed to beat just about the entire Harrow team before coolly slotting past the keeper. It was pure poetry from a player not used to performing in poetic mode.

I have said much about the managerial era of Pete Cherry. Sadly he left the club in controversial circumstances, convinced that there was a boardroom plot to 'send him upstairs' and be replaced by Steve Richardson.

Cherry finally resigned and was indeed replaced by Rico. But it was a short stay.

Garry Wilson's arrival after being madly sacked by Hastings in February, 1999, and the appointment of Nick Greenwood as head coach was to take the club to new levels. The Cherry years were magic. The Wilson and Nick Greenwood show has been awesome.

Nobody but nobody could have predicted the heights to which they were to take the club.

After winning the county league in style and a first season in the Dr Martens League, Langney Sports were given a new name, Eastbourne Borough.

This was no easy decision for the committee for whom the name of Langney Sports had special sentimental value.

A group of supporters refused to accept the change and I criticised them for continuing their Langney Sports chants.

Let's face it, the new name of Eastbourne Borough made the club easily identifiable throughout the country and made the club more readily acceptable to sponsors.

Since then the name of Eastbourne Borough has become known and respected throughout the world of non league football and beyond.

Under Wilson and Greenwood, promotion has followed promotion leaving the club where Len Smith and his committee had once feared to tread.

Whoever would have thought that the unknown team competing in park football three decades ago would today be facing, in league games, the likes of Oxford United, Wrexham, Torquay, Cambridge United and Mansfield? And in 2009-10, Luton Town were added to that list.

Wilson and Greenwood have been the miracle workers at Priory Lane. An FA Cup draw at home to Oxford in 2005 attracted nearly 4,000 fans to a ground where at one time 500 would have been regarded as a bumper attendance.

Borough lost the replay 3-0 but so good were the performances of striker Yemi Odubade that Oxford later snapped him up for a transfer fee that was to put £25,000 into the club coffers.

There have been so many great moments during this unique club's unbelievable existence. But surely the greatest was in May, 2008 when Borough beat Hampstead & Richmond 2-0 in the play-off final at Stevenage to seal a place in the Conference National.

It was a night of champagne and glory and one which Garry Wilson described as "the best moment of my career."

But with the glory came fresh hurdles to climb. Journeys to places as far away as Barrow, made huge demands on the balance sheet.

A new pay deal was negotiated for the players with the accent on appearances and performances. Needless to say, Borough took time to adapt to a whole new ball game. But adapt they did, pulling off momentous victories against Torquay United, Stevenage and Kettering to name but a few.

Len Smith estimated the club needed to average 1,000 fans a game to break even. Borough ended their debut Blue Square Premier season several hundred in excess of this figure and well ahead of their Sussex rivals Crawley and Lewes.

I have mentioned players, I have mentioned Len Smith, but behind the scenes chief executive Mike Spooner has won numerous awards for the club programme and former Chelsea chief executive Colin Hutchinson has brought a wealth of experience to the boardroom, with Oxford 'signing' Lorna Gosling as commercial manager winning the hearts and minds of many prospective sponsors.

The best, however, I have left to last. At the time of writing, defender Darren Baker was approaching 850 first team appearances for the club.

He has performed throughout the glory years from County League to Conference National. Each year, the cynics ask, "Will this be his last season?'

But so far, Baker has proved them wrong with unbelievable consistency in Borough's often watertight defence.

Baker is a true legend in an amazing club for which no hurdle appears too tough, despite a challenging second season at the top of the non-league pyramid .

18 A little bit of Eric

WHEN the appointment was announced of Peter Lindsey as group editor of the Eastbourne Gazette & Herald, there were rumblings among the editorial team at Commercial Road.

Lindsey had edited the Crawley Observer and the Sussex Express in his early twenties. At the time there had been much criticism of MD Mike Pakes for entrusting the editorial chair to a relatively inexperienced young man.

A local referee renowned for showing players red cards, Lindsey also had a reputation for making those who worked under him see red.

I first met him after he had officiated at an Eastbourne United match and although I criticised him for his performance that day, he took it in good heart.

I had always got on well with PL and on my first official meeting with him after he became editor at Eastbourne, I was delighted when he said he was more than happy with the sports pages.

Lindsey was renowned for his banter which was loved by some and loathed by others. He loved nothing more than winding people up. Some of his ways took me back to the days of Eric Redfern.

Lindsey had 10 eventful years at Eastbourne making friends and enemies. There were criticisms of his abilities as a sub and, like me, he struggled with new technology.

His achievements, however, were considerable. He presided over controversial papers with booming circulations, brilliantly leading a campaign highlighting the bizarre goings-on at the District General Hospital. His highly successful Achievers Nights - at which I was honoured to receive the Sports Personality of the Year award following my retirement - was one of many events instigated by him which raised thousands of pounds for charity.

His move back to Hastings was finally ordered by regional MD Michael Johnston, much to Lindsey's anguish at the time.

To those who complained most about PL I used to say: "You should have worked under Eric Redfern!" In many ways the two were similar, but you could always talk to PL and he would hear you out. Like Redfern, PL will not be forgotten.

Peter Austin following Peter Lindsey was akin to Hugh Rowlings following Eric Redfern. Chalk and cheese.

Austin was a rarity in local journalism in that as well as being an editor, he had been a production director and an MD.

Added to that he is one of nicest guys anyone could wish to meet, masterly at man management and equally well versed whether in print or editorial matters.

When he started his editorship at Eastbourne he could surely not have foreseen the abruptness with which it was to end, his early retirement being due to a cutback in editors required by Johnston Press in the East Sussex area.

19 Our England cricketers

ALTHOUGH the feats of Eastbourne Cricket Club have twice provided memorable days at Lord's with victory and defeat in the national cup finals, it has been Eastbourne's two England cricketers who have dominated the back pages over the last decade.

James Kirtley and Ed Giddins are two excellent pace bowlers who both appear on the coveted honours board at Lord's, having taken five wickets or more during a Test match.

The pair have constantly attracted the attentions of national newspaper journalists for very different reasons.

Kirtley, who continues to take wickets for Sussex, has been to hell and back in a bid to get his bowling action accepted by the authorities.

The action of the Sussex paceman has been under close scrutiny since he was first reported by Colonel Naudshad Ali during England's tour of Zimbabwe in October 2001.

Kirtley had agreed to send me regular bulletins of his first England adventure which turned terribly sour when the legitimacy of his action was called into serious question as Ali reported him after he had taken 2-33 on his one-day international debut.

The irony was that Kirtley had already been cleared by the ICC after remedial work and was forced to have further sessions with former England bowling coach Bob Cottam before he was cleared for a second time.

Kirtley has shown amazing character over the years by his refusal to be beaten by the so-called experts and provided us all with a day to savour when he was named man-of-the-match after spearheading an England victory against South Africa in 2002.

I can well remember updating the Herald back page as I watched, on the office TV, Kirtley take an amazing 6-34 on his Test debut.

The next morning he was back page headlines in every national newspaper, but he still found time to phone me at the office and let me know how rightly proud he was of such an extraordinary feat witnessed and admired by the world of cricket.

Kirtley represented England in three more Test matches but I believe he was never given a fair deal by the England selectors.

My coverage of Ed Giddins was very much in contrast to that of Kirtley for the simple reason they are two hugely different characters.

Yes, they are both world class pacemen, but there the similarity ends. Kirtley is the serious diplomat, the perfect ambassador for England, particularly abroad.

While Kirtley fell foul of the law because of his bowling action, Giddins was involved in far more sinister misdemeanours. The former Eastbourne College student was the town's first ever Test cricketer, being chosen for England after he had been sacked by Sussex for drug offences and banned from first-class cricket for 18 months.

That was in 1996 Seven years later he was fined £5,000 and banned from cricket for a further five years after being found guilty of placing a £7,000 bet on his own Surrey side to lose a Championship match.

The burly bowler made his international debut against New Zealand in August, 1999 and bowled superbly to take 4-79. In the two Tests against Zimbabwe the following summer his magnificent 5-15 in the first Zimbabwe innings was a key factor in swinging the match in England's favour. Giddins also took two wickets in the second innings but made only one more appearance for England in the opening game of a five-match Test series against West Indies, taking 0-73 in a game England lost by an innings.

On a sad note, we were robbed in July, 2009, of one of the best-loved men I have known in the world of local sport. Peter Bibby was a great Eastbourne batsman in the '70s and '80s, but it was his work for the youth section of the Saffrons that could not be measured. Many brilliant young cricketers owe their success to him including six of Eastbourne's senior side who won the national Cup at Lord's in 1997.

It was typical of Peter that he battled asbestos-related lung cancer without a word of complaint. The Saffrons will not be the same without him.

20 Premiership sadness

JOHN Piercy was Eastbourne's one and only Premiership footballer. He grew up with Old Town Boys Club, was selected for the England youth team and was given a four-year contract by Spurs. He moved to Brighton before colitis sadly ended his soccer career at the age of 25.

I first saw Piercy play at Wembley when he was just 11, helping Ocklynge School win the national Smiths Crisps soccer tournament.

It was not only a big match for Piercy, but also Gareth Connolly, who was in his early teens and covering the match photographically for the Eastbourne Herald.

While John Piercy celebrated victory, it was a day of both joy and heartbreak for his dad Dave, for 25 years the chairman of Old Town Boys. Dave was hugely proud of his son's Wembley appearance but was unable to make the journey as he was in hospital with colitis, the very illness which was to cut short his son's career.

John was a schoolboy star who seemed destined for a great future. A striker or attacking midfielder, he was thrilled to be given a four-year contract with Spurs, despite being an avid Arsenal supporter. He made his Spurs debut against Crewe in the Worthington Cup and in eight league appearances went on to face such teams as Arsenal, Manchester United, Chelsea and Liverpool.

He signed for Brighton after being released by Spurs in 2002. I recall speaking to him after he had his Brighton contract extended by the then manager Mark McGhee just days before getting married. 'It was the best wedding present I could have had," he said.

A couple of years later he had split up from his wife and had been forced to take early retirement from the game he loved.

Sometimes you wonder – just how cruel can life be?

Piercy has since provided us with some magic moments at the Saffrons. Sadly, he failed to start the 2009 season. But local soccer fans will certainly hope they have not seen the last of him, either releasing an inch-perfect defence-splitting pass or finding the back of the net from 25 yards.

Piercy was the jewel in Eastbourne's soccer crown.

Epilogue

ALL good things come to an end. My innings in local journalism just failed to carry me to the half-century mark. But it was a near thing - 48½ years of continuous employment; I am not complaining.

Sadly, others have not been so lucky. Over nearly half a century I have seen good friends from the production staff as well as editorial colleagues fall by the wayside.

When my journalistic life began at Bexhill in 1960, nobody had heard of the word redundancy. In the printing industry, many a son succeeded his father whether as a typesetter or compositor.

Their unions were strong and, with bonuses and overtime, they generally took home a considerably larger wage packet than the average journalist.

The majority of newspapers were printed at premises where the editorial operation was also carried out, the Hastings and Bexhill Observers in Cambridge Road and the Eastbourne papers in Pevensey Road, later in Commercial Road.

There were day and night shifts of type-setters and compositors on duty around the clock. The advances of new technology, however, were to put these workers out of a job.

A number of journalistic positions also went during the recession of the early nineties, but nothing compared with the recession of 2009 which has had a devastating affect on the newspaper industry.

Who would ever have thought that the spring of 2009 would see no receptionists at Eastbourne, one staff photographer (down from six when I started) and the sub-editing of the papers being carried out at Portsmouth with one editor responsible for all the newspapers at Eastbourne, Bexhill and Hastings?

Who could possibly have forecast that Eastbourne editor Peter Austin would have taken retirement nearly five years early and his predecessor Peter Lindsey (latterly editor at Hastings) made redundant in the prime of his journalistic life?

Later in 2009 came news of yet another new computer system in which reporters would write their stories directly onto the page and create their own headline. The unheard-of seemed likely to happen – newspapers without sub-editors.

As everyone who has worked in journalism knows, long hours are part and parcel of newspaper life. In sport particularly, many people's leisure time is working hours for journalists. And if you are very fortunate there is a patient wife waiting for you when you come home.

During Tennis Week, I have arrived home as late as 4am on a Thursday morning and been back in the office five hours later.

I have been one of the exceptionally lucky ones. In February, 1975, I married Kathy, taking on and adopting her three children Roger, Angela and Richard.

We were an immediate happy family, one that was extended with the arrival of Kevin in August, 1980 and Karen in April, 1983. What an unforgettable April that was – the birth of Karen, later to become a gifted beauty therapist with her own business in Bexhill – and Brighton & Hove Albion reaching the FA Cup final for the first and only time in their history. I was privileged to be at both events.

I am proud of each and every member of my family and to Kathy I am everlastingly grateful for her support through thick and thin. It was indeed a magical day when, in my retirement year, we renewed our wedding vows under the blue skies of St. Lucia.

My thanks at the end of a memorable innings go to her, my children, my always supportive sister Joan and brother-in-law Jacques, editors who have supported me, sports deputies who have given their all and office colleagues who have put up with me with such good humour over the years.

Three Men and a Quote
Part 2

The John Dowling Story

JOHN Dowling was born in his parents' bungalow at Church Vale Road, Bexhill-on-Sea, on September 29th, 1944, the only child of Percy and Grace Dowling. He attended the former St Peter's Church of England Infants and Junior Schools in Barrack Road before entering the Technical Department of the Down County Secondary School for Boys in the town. He joined the Bexhill Observer in August, 1961 as a school leaver and served a five-year apprenticeship as a junior reporter. After a spell as chief reporter, he was appointed deputy editor in 1974. Like Philip Elms and Ken McEwan, John had opportunities to work on larger papers but opted for the job satisfaction of involvement in his hometown community. John met his wife Ann through her work as mayor's secretary to the former Bexhill Borough Council. Their son Paul and his wife Mel have rewarded them with granddaughters Molly and Rosie. John took voluntary early retirement in February, 2009 when the provincial newspaper industry was badly hit by the international recession. He continues to live in his beloved Bexhill and remains committed to a number of community organisations.

1 Uncertain Beginnings

YOU called him "Sir." His rule was absolute. You incurred his displeasure at your peril. Being called to the editor's office was akin to being summoned to the headmaster's study.

I stood on the threadbare rug which, in an otherwise lino-covered editorial environment, was a symbol of exalted rank. I awaited my fate.

It was early days. I was still under evaluation to see if I had the potential to be offered an apprenticeship.

I had transgressed. Charged with interviewing one of the Old Man's dearest Masonic chums and his wife on their golden wedding I had omitted one thing - to break it to the Old Man that his pals had not wanted to know the Observer's representatives and had shut the door on the photographer and yours truly.

Now, minutes before deadline, the editor had in front of him his beloved page lay-out sheet. At the top of the page was an ominous hole. He expected interviews to be in depth. He specialised, particularly the case of his pals, in filling a broadsheet page with a bedsheet-sized picture.

Now he had neither. And I had failed to warn him. The big clock on his office wall was ticking. But my heart was beating faster and louder.

The three of us have long since appreciated how much we owe to Len Bartley's tough but thorough training in journalism. He was a seasoned campaigner with countless tricks of the trade to impart.

But he didn't suffer fools gladly.

The Old Man offered the world two facial expressions. One was comparatively benign. The other featured gimlet eyes.

If he addressed you, gimlet-eyed, as "old boy…" you were in doubly-deep trouble.

"Look, *old boy...*" he had begun. This school-leaver, the lowest form of editorial life, a £6-a-week "cub" reporter, felt his stomach tighten in a sudden spasm of Headmaster Syndrome.

Eventually, the tirade ended; not with the cane but with the stern warning: "Do that again and I'll *bollock* you!"

In my adolescent innocence I truly expected to be the recipient of a kick in the crotch.

Suddenly the expression "to go hot under the collar" took on an all-too-real significance. I was not just hot in that region. It felt as if I were burning.

Dismissed with an angry wave of the hand, I turned to go. As I did I happened to glance upward. There, over the Old Man's door, was his other symbol of journalistic office.

He was the proud owner of an infra-red electric heater. It glowered as malevolently at me as the Old Man had done.

This then was the world of journalism I had entered shortly before my 17th birthday - the calling for which I had aimed single-mindedly since the age of eight when I had reasoned that, good at English and abysmal at maths, it offered my best chance of scraping a living while at the same time extracting some job satisfaction from the process.

Had I made a mistake?

Years later, after beginning what was to be a tragically brief retirement, the Old Man paid me a visit in my office as deputy editor. During conversation he revealed the philosophy behind his managerial approach.

"You know, you are not *really* in charge of a newspaper until you have read your name on the shithouse wall."

Sage word, as always, from Len Bartley to whom I owe a great deal for a strict but thorough editorial training.

2 Why journalism?

WITH his customary wisdom, the Old Man had fired a warning shot across my bows at my job interview. "I suppose you are a school prefect?" editor Leonard Bartley asked, a little pointedly I thought. I replied with some pride that I was.

Had I won any prizes at Speech Day? Well, yes, I had...

"It will be very different here. You won't be at the top. You will be at the bottom of the pile, old boy...."

He made it clear that if he took me on it would be as the lowest form of life in a busy working office. If I made the grade he would consider taking me on as an apprentice with the giddying prospect of five years on rock-bottom wages.

If I did not live up to his expectations and those of former teacher Rex Salter, who had evidently put in a good word for me, I could expect to be shown the door - in the same way as the lad I was replacing.

How had I got to this point? Why was I here in this intimidating presence? In short, why journalism as a career?

Looking back, I suppose the idea took root when I was about eight. In those days "essay" writing was an important part of the school curriculum. Working on the proven carrot-and-stick theory, teachers would read out to the rest of the class a small selection of the essays they considered worthy of some childish merit.

The carrot-and-stick worked. It became a matter of some pride to have one's work read to the rest of the class. An element of friendly competition developed between a few of us. By the time we got to Miss Brocklehurst's class at the top of the old St Peter's Junior School in Barrack Road, a bookish lad named Ian Thomas was my principal rival.

For Miss Brocklehurst to have fired-up any form of industry in me was, in retrospect, a monumental achievement. I have never possessed a competitive nature.

"Bet I can race you to the end of the road!" This type of boyhood challenge produced no response whatever.

If someone thought he could run faster than me then good luck to him. It was a matter of supreme indifference to me. I had brought idleness to off to a fine art, contriving to do the least work possible at school consistent with keeping out of serious trouble.

You knew when you were in serious trouble at primary school in those days. That was when the teacher used BOTH your names - not just your Christian name.

"John Dowling!" Miss Winifred Reeve was headmistress. She was a no-nonsense Lancastrian. And she had got my measure to a nicety.

She timed her warning to perfection - in Assembly, when my embarrassment and discomfort would be in front of the whole school and not just my classmates to whom my idleness was no novelty.

"John Dowling! Do you know what I am going to write in your report for your parents to read...?"

Daft question. How should I know what she was going to write in my soppy old report?

"I'm going to write *'lethargic'.*"

Miss Reeve imbued the word with a terrible menace. It was a measure designed to frighten me out of my laziness.

"There is only one way I am not going to put 'lethargic' in your report, John Dowling, and that is if you can tell me what it means!"

It was true. I *was* lethargic. But it was a focussed form of lethargy. There were some very specific aspects of school work for which I made an exception.

Essay-writing, as we have seen, was one. Another was history, which I have always loved. A third was reading. Though the school library system then consisted of a wooden trunk which appeared at regular intervals and into which keener readers plunged with a desperation born of real hunger, I spent a lot of my leisure time with my head in a book. And I *loved* words.

"Well, John Dowling? What does 'lethargic' mean then…?"

The Assembly was hushed. How was Dopey Dowling going to wriggle out of this one?

"Please Miss, I think of it as 'economy of effort…'"

I gulped at my own audacity and hoped to get off without lines or detention.

"You were always too smart for your own good, John Dowling!"

But, of course, Miss Reeve kept her word. "Lethargic" did not appear in that term's report.

There were plenty of other opportunities to put across the same point to my folks, who were assured at parents' evenings that, though considered bright, I was something of a disappointment.

Over-confident and still a devotee of "economy of effort," I was among those who though they passed Eleven Plus were not accorded a grammar school place.

"You'll be a square peg in a round hole…" Miss Reeve admonished as I left to take a place at what one of my new teachers delighted in referring to as "the Poor Boys' Eton."

Officially, it was the Technical stream at the Down County Secondary School for Boys. But to former journalist Rex Salter, my form-teacher in Class One and later my history master, the strictly-segregated boys' school was simply the counterpart of "the Poor Girls' Roedean" next door!

Rex employed humour as a valuable educational tool. In those happily pre-PC days when nicknames could be accorded by teachers to pupils and corporal punishment was the accepted norm, Rex (Old Spit and Dribble to us lads) made lessons fun.

Roger Barfoot set a lead in grasping the principles of decimals. He became "Decimal Dan" in Rex's parlance. Rodney Hobden, the class mathematician, was "Euclid."

But it was not all fun and games. Rex wielded both cane and slipper with punishing effect.

Thus: "Watch it, Blondie, or I'll get Smiler out!" translated as a warning to the blond-haired Barry Henderson that another wise-crack from the back-row would be rewarded by Rex getting his cane out of the cupboard.

Smiler was his cane. Grouser was a plimsol of truly Salterian proportions - the sole worn smooth by its application to boys' backsides.

"Smiler" could be applied to the backside or, more memorably, to the palm of the hand. I was both caned and slippered by Rex, usually for talking in class.

But, like Miss Brocklehurst before him, Rex coaxed and encouraged my better side, developing my love of writing and of literature.

It was a process developed further on the next stage of my school journey by my next English teacher, Malcolm Pratt. Malcolm's was an altogether gentler form of humour. He would wait with a patient half-smile until class comedian Roger "Tub" Bechter got to the stage-whispered punch-line of a gag.

The lid of Malcolm's desk would rise. Shoulders shaking with mirth, he would delve inside. We *swore* he wrote down the punch-line of Tub's better offerings before reaching for his cane.

To Malcolm, as to Mildred Brocklehurst (later Spencer), to Rex and, latterly, deputy head Maurice Middleton I owe a huge debt of gratitude for fostering the one aspect of my academic life where I displayed some promise and - more significantly - applied some effort.

Each of them read to us on a regular basis. It is, in my view, an educational tool the impact of which is hugely under-valued. My enduring love of Kenneth Grahame's children's classic, The

Wind In The Willows, I owe to Miss Brocklehurst. Much more was to follow.

Parents attending pre-admission interviews at the Poor Boys' Eton, had to promise that in return for their lads' inclusion in the school's top "T" (technical) stream, they would allow them to stay on the then voluntary "extra" year and sit GCE 0-Level examinations in Class Five.

These were the Fifties. For many working class parents like my own, that extra year of schooling was a costly sacrifice.

It is a measure of how times have since changed that few boys went on to take A-levels. This meant making the transition to the grammar school, which possessed a sixth form.

From memory, only one boy in our year at the Down went to university, though several took degrees later as mature students.

This is no reflection on standards at the Down. Headmaster Ramsay Nicholson was in many respects an educational pioneer. The bluntly- outspoken Scot was known to hammer the table at county hall as he campaigned for better resources.

He fought a long and tough battle both at county hall and in the staffroom to create homework classes. He recognised that many homes lacked somewhere for lads to concentrate on their homework away from the distractions of siblings or the new-fangled television.

He persuaded staff to double-up time spent marking classwork with supervising homework. School ended at 3.45pm. We had until 4pm to munch a few sandwiches before returning to the classroom. In theory, by 6pm one could go home with the day's work completed.

Then as now, good jobs were hard to find in Bexhill. Many of my contemporaries chose a career in the armed forces. Others sought apprenticeships in industry or took up teacher-training.

It is to the everlasting credit of the team that Ramsay Nicholson led that so many lads went on from The Down to outstanding careers. "Nick," as I later discovered, kept a proud and careful track of their progress, displaying incredible diligence in the process.

As decision-time approached for our class, I incurred the displeasure of the county careers service by adopting an independent path. Rex Salter had trained as a journalist with the old Bexhill Chronicle, a rival paper later absorbed into the Observer as a victim of the Great Depression. Rex was enjoying a career as an evening newspaper reporter by the time that war interrupted. When eventually he came out of the RAF, having served as a navigator, he opted to take one of the training courses created to cope with the post-war demand for teachers.

But he never fully abandoned his first-love and still worked as a freelance sports reporter for the Observer.

It was Rex who tipped me off that the Observer was seeking a school-leaver and Rex who had put in that good word for me with editor Len Bartley.

It was enough to get me a start as the editorial team's "lowest form of life."

And despite those early misgivings when I incurred the Old Man's wrath, I have never regretted it.

Nor have I ever ceased to be grateful to successive teachers who encouraged me to write.

3 Isaac Pitman

THE concept of being a member of a minority group comes easily when you are an only child. From boyhood you know you are "different" and think little of it as a consequence.

"John, is it *not* possible for you to use your right hand?" The voice was that of Miss Peirce (mature single ladies in those days tended not to reveal their first names - and one didn't ask).

In an age before block-release college courses became the industry norm, my generation (though not Phil's) learnt their craft by the "Aunt Nelly Method."

This may be loosely defined as "Aunt Nelly does it this way, so just do the same and stop asking stupid questions."

Until the dawn of the era when we were sent on day-release to Brighton College, private tuition from good souls such as Miss Peirce was the norm. Miss Peirce had premises in the road running parallel to the office. She had been teaching shorthand there since before the War. Certainly her text books were of that vintage.

She was a good, diligent, soul who taught us well. She was strict, but not unfriendly. In retrospect, I can see that the tuition she gave me has served me well. But I didn't conform to the expected norm. And that caused problems for both of us.

In addition to being an only-child, colour-blind and short-sighted, I am also left-handed.

When you are left-handed *nothing* fits. You get used to the fact that scissors cut into your hands with greater effectiveness than they cut paper, for example.

Shorthand posed still greater problems. Miss Peirce returned to her theme.

"Are you sure you can't use your right hand? Isaac Pitman designed his system for right-handers..."

Well, he would, wouldn't he? *Everything* is designed for the majority. We minority groups just have to learn to live with it.

And so I had to adapt Isaac Pitman's wonderful system to my own needs.

Pitman shorthand is designed so the right-handed elite can *draw* upward strokes – as opposed to *pushing* them. It might seem a minor point. But when you are attempting to work at speed it assumes a new dimension.

The system is designed so the outlines flow easily from one to the other.

Left-handers trail behind in this respect.

The one-to-one (sometimes two-to-one if Mac accompanied me) tuition from Miss Peirce was, of course, excellent.

But there was an added disadvantage. Because her text books and exercises came out of the commercial Ark, we were taking down such antediluvian passages as: "Dear sir, I am in receipt of your favour of the 21st instant…"

The exercises included many such outlines we would seldom encounter in practice. Worse, they contained few of the words we would be taking constantly at court and council and the rest of the weekly round.

When the transfer came to the college at Brighton we fondly hoped that we would be on a different dictation wavelength. The first day was a disappointment.

"Dear Sir, I am in receipt of your favour…"

Like Miss Peirce, the college was long accustomed to training compliant future shorthand typists. Argumentative cub reporters seeking something more suited to their needs posed a problem which was apparently insoluble.

The college had never undertaken a journalism course before. None of the lecturers had ever been a journalist. It was farcical.

I never did take my Proficiency Test.

What I did find is that there is a *world* of difference between taking dictation in class and note-taking in the real world.

For a start, dictation passages were carefully graded in increasing difficulty and speed but were of short duration and read with clarity and care.

Then as now, council meetings at Bexhill Town Hall began at 6.30pm. The borough system with committee meetings closed to press and public was very different to today's district council with its leader-and-cabinet system.

The latter channels almost everything of importance into the single decision-making cabinet, where the majority group presents a carefully pre-choreographed approximation of debate. Dissent is rare.

The borough system with its constant points of order interruptions and references back fostered debate. The council meeting was an opportunity for the opposing political parties to play to what was usually a well-supported, knowledgeable and hyper-critical public gallery.

The system nurtured orators, some mediocre, others outstandingly able, but all with no concept of brevity.

Trained to take shorthand in five-minute exercises at a regulated speed, council (and court) were dauntingly different for a faltering apprentice.

Late nights were the norm. The longest – 6.30pm to 1am - did not come until Rother days. But that is another story. Rother were debating sacking their own chief executive.

An added complication for the likes of Mac and myself was that the old man *always* sat in at borough council meetings.

Worse, he carried a fistful of plain postcards. Using his own devastatingly quick Pitman, he would make the odd note on the cards.

Such was the detail in which we were expected to cover every debate, that Mac and I took to writing-up the previous night's meeting together in the peace and quiet of Mac's parents' home.

To bash out 80 single-paragraph "slips" on a single debate was not unusual.

Inevitably, no matter how extensive our note-taking or how generously we had quoted the speakers, the Old Man took on that gimlet-eyed look as he read through our lengthy stories.

Use of the expression "Old Boy" meant, as usual, deep trouble.

"Look, *old boy,* I take it you did get dear old Councillor Bloggs' quote on..."

Dear old Councillor Bloggs was inevitably one of his Masonic chums. The Old Man did not relish being questioned on his juniors' failings when he attended Lodge meetings.

Is it any wonder that under later editorships I was accused of over-writing?

Bearing in mind that the Observer was still a broadsheet paper, Len Bartley's advice when asked what length of story he wanted tells all.

"No need to over-write it, old boy. Just a quick two columns for the front and we can turn the rest inside..."

And all this taking Pitman with the "wrong" hand...

*There is a footnote to the Pitman-learning era. Len Bartley frequently spoke with affection and profound respect of an old colleague called Harry Butler.

We knew of Harry Butler solely because he was the man who *set* the shorthand examinations in Pitman – and in Gregg and new-fangled T-Line.

Harry Butler was a *god* to us. He had an encyclopaedic knowledge of all three systems and had arguably the fastest speed of any living being.

The phone rang in the Western Road office. "Harry Butler here..."

The Harry Butler..?

Was Len there? No, sorry, he's on leave. Pity. Harry was staying for a couple of nights at the Granville Hotel and had been hoping to chat about old times.

Clearly, it was going to be a lonely evening for him.

"What are you doing, this evening? Would you join me for dinner?"

This was a daunting prospect indeed. He sensed my reticence.

"I promise not to ask to see your notebook."

I accepted. And, of course, Harry eventually persuaded me to hand over the offending shorthand notes.

"I see you've developed your own short-forms." These are even quicker ways of note-taking, consisting of blending two or more outlines into one.

Harry was not dismissive. Rather, he was encouraging – and appreciative of my handicap,

"That short-form is a good idea.

"Of course, you could shorten it further – like this, and this, and this."

That after-dinner chat was a revelation.

Thank you, Harry, wherever you are 45 years on. This left-hander still uses a little of the immense number of wonderful ideas you imparted that night.

4 The Chubby Checker

IT would happen every few days. Without fail. An acrid smell would develop and we would all look to see the pall of smoke rising from reporter Gavin Hardman-Brown's wastepaper basket.

Inevitably, Gavin had knocked his pipe out in the basket and ignited the balls of screwed-up copy paper. In the Sixties when reporters were still free to smoke in offices such occurrences hardly caused a raised eyebrow.

Had he smoked, Bob Quayle would never have had this problem. War between Len Bartley as editor and Bob as sub-editor was constant and vicious.

Bob was usually the butt of the Old Man's bile at the Saturday morning "inquest" into that week's paper.

The two men had totally different approaches to the job. Poor Bob couldn't help being pedantic. When I wrote in a wedding report that the happy couple had left for a honeymoon in New York aboard the Queen Mary he queried: "Do you mean the famous ship…?"

Len Bartley was equally meticulous and exacting but got so exasperated at Bob's continual re-writes that he took to going through Bob's wastepaper basket after work and confronting him with the offending screwed-up copy paper in the morning.

Bob continued to re-write - but stuffed the resultant wads of copy paper into his pockets. At the end of a working day he would swing a leg over the saddle of his old push-bike and ride off towards Glenleigh Park and his supper looking like the Michelin Man.

Bob was a kindly, if sometimes exasperating, man. It was he who when John Liddle, then a fellow Junior, became paralytic at an office Christmas party offered him a lift home.

Bob had driven to work that day in his trusty 100E Ford. But instead of driving John directly to Down Road, he took him to the top of Galley Hill, Bexhill's low cliff. There he had set him out in the cold night air and driven off slowly with John jogging behind.

Bexhill's restorative sea "breeze" soon had John sober enough to be taken to his parents' home. Matters changed dramatically after Bob's retirement. Mike Storr-Hoggins came to the Observer from Cornwall. Initially, he and the editor got on well.

But the honeymoon didn't last. Mike was not a man to endure the old man's acid tongue.

Mike had suffered a fearful motorcycle accident before coming to Sussex. His forehead bore the outward scars. He had a spectacularly short fuse as a result.

I missed the show-down. I was out of the office when Mike threatened to "crown" the Old Man with a typewriter. Len Bartley reportedly shot down the back stairs to the refuge of works manager "Rowie" Reeve's ground-floor office after bellowing: "instant dismissal!"

Roy Jones was round and jolly; good company but an equally meticulous "sub". His mantra to young reporters who were expected to get all facts verified before submitting copy was "Check! Check! And check again!"

The Twist was the dance craze of the time. Inevitably, Roy was dubbed "The Chubby Checker."

John Swift had been chief revise sub on the Rand Daily Mail. When an old aunt left him a house in Barrack Road he took the opportunity to get out of Hendrick Verwoerd's apartheid-ridden regime before his outspoken indignation at its racist extremes got him into further trouble.

He was not only a genial character but a highly-experienced and able sub-editor.

His ability to envisage and lay out a page at speed was remarkable. It also got the pair of us in trouble.

Len Bartley was, himself, a very able newsman. In his days with the Peterborough Evening Telegraph he had prided himself on his ability to have the sports edition, "the Old Pink'un," on the streets with the match result virtually as football fans left the stadium.

Every newspaper needs a re-launch once in a while, a kind of spring-clean to freshen it up and so boost circulation. Len had been brought in during the early Fifties to give the Bexhill Observer a make-over. His introduction of page lay-outs annoyed the stone-hands at Hastings, who had been used to lobbing in stories in virtually whichever order they chose.

Len rather resented John's abilities and when I came up with a particularly hot story and John did one of his lightning-fast lay-out responses things came to a head.

A contact had tipped me off about a child-murder. Always an early-riser, I had gone to the old Cantelupe Road police station and got the first facts of the case ahead of anyone else.

By 8am I was knocking on John's door to tell him. We needed to strip out the planned front page and replace our lead story. John could picture his planned page in his head. His pencil sped over the proverbial back of an envelope at the breakfast table - story here, picture there and above them a large and graphic headline.

Looking back with maturity, I suppose that in the adrenalin-rush of the moment my mistake was to burst into Len's office, gabble through my murder story and John's breakfast response to it and present him with a Page One *fait accompli.*

Bexhill is a conservative town. Successive editors have had to adjust to the style of journalism to which the Observer's readership approve.

Len, who had suffered sad personal loss in his family life, erred on the side of caution. He didn't like the bold tell-it-like-it-is front page with which he had been confronted. He demanded that it be toned-down. We argued that Observer readers would want to know what had happened, no matter how unpalatable and tragic.

There was a stormy stand-off at the end of which I alluded to an incident at Len's previous paper at Kings Lynn when staff gave management a virtual "him or us" ultimatum which had not gone in his favour.

It was unpleasant. I hated doing it. A compromise solution saw a somewhat watered-down banner headline.

But Observer readers got their front page murder story.

In 1974 John Liddle, who had transferred to our sister paper, the Sussex Express and County Herald and then to the Eastbourne Herald, returned to Bexhill as editor following Len Bartley's retirement.

John did for the Observer in the Seventies what Len had done in the Fifties. With me as his deputy, we did another re-launch. It was the start of a happy, but sadly brief, period during which this old friendship and the introduction of some new blood from the Eastbourne Herald took the Observer into a new era.

It also took us into new premises. The Observer had been in the ownership of the Parsons family newspaper group since its foundation in May 1896.

Suddenly, we were owned by Morgan Grampian. They wanted Parsons' lucrative Travel Trade Gazette and having got it, promptly sold us on to Westminster Press. "Asset-strippers" were then very much in company vogue.

But Morgan Grampian retained the old Western Road buildings. The print works closed, The clatter in the letterpress hall ceased. Printing machines stood out on the forecourt awaiting either new owners or the scrap metal man. Staff either transferred to the Hastings works or lost their jobs.

Editorial did a hurried and very DIY move round the corner to Sackville Road. This followed an argument with the town hall over the council's insistence that on-site parking should be provided. The firm paid into a corporate fund which was supposed eventually to pay for an off-street car park for the town.

That car park was never to materialise, by the way!

In swift order, what had been a ladies' hairdressing salon in Sackville Road was converted to our use. So hasty was the conversion that for years advertising clients were received in what were still quite obviously salon cubicles. Upstairs, a maisonette became the editorial offices.

There was no room to accommodate bound editions of the Observer going back to 1896 or those of the Bexhill Chronicle which from 1887 until its take-over by the Observer in 1931 was the Observer's rival.

I brokered the files' extended loan to Bexhill Library, giving the public access to them for the first time and ridding us of a storage problem. Reference librarian Roger Bristow and I carted them down Western Road in a trolley borrowed from the print works!

Sadly, the public abused the privilege of free access to the files. Told it was not possible to take photo-copies from them without breaking the fragile binding, unscrupulous researchers took to slicing out stories with a razor blade, doing irreversible harm. It was a relief when in 2007 the Library needed the space for its refurbishment and I brokered a further extended loan to Bexhill Museum where a closer eye could be kept on them.

Many true and lasting friendships were generated in nearly five decades of reporting.

Bill Sansom was a long-serving Bexhill Borough councillor who, following defeat at the polls, was made an Alderman. He was mayor several times, chaired the Bexhill, Battle and Rye Committee which mapped out the future pattern when local government reorganisation imposed an unpopular merger between the three towns and was chairman of resultant Rother District Council for its first two formative years.

That friendship weathered many storms.

One of the earliest came in the memorably cold winter of 1962-1963. The snow was so thick and remained so long that road-clearance by the borough council - or rather the lack of it - became a town scandal.

Colleague Beryl Parker and I covered a borough council meeting together at which both Bill as highways committee chairman and Alan Geldard as borough surveyor came under intense fire.

To be fair to them, the conditions were the worst since 1947. No wonder the town was ill-prepared. They defended themselves robustly and argued that although the borough had got off to a slow start, snow ploughs had been fitted to lorries and the roads had at last been cleared.

Alan lived in Millfield Rise, not a quarter mile from the town hall. Bill offered to give him a lift on the "snow-free" but still-slippery roads. Wisely, I had walked. Beryl and I had got as far as the junction of Amherst Road with Mitten Road when we spotted one of the only cars that were out on such a night.

It was Bill's. And it was stuck in a pile of hard-frozen snow in the centre of the junction.

Bill had just started to appeal "Give us a push, please..." when he saw who the two figures were.

"Don't you dare report this!"

Now would we ...?

By 1978 Rother was in deep trouble which ended with it becoming the first of the newly-created districts to remove its own chief executive.

It was a time of rumour and counter-rumour, of plot and counter-plot. In a rare example of us coming to blows, Bill phoned the office after one particular disclosure and demanded to know who the Town Hall "mole" was.

A good journalist never discloses his sources. Bill, Conservative group leader, became still more annoyed. "I'll find that mole and when I do so I will deal with them severely," he roared.

I quietly explained that practically everyone on the council, himself included, were or had been "moles" when they thought the occasion demanded it.

By far the greatest piece of good fortune that working on the Observer brought me was meeting my wife. Ann was mayor's secretary. In those days the Observer either rang to inquire about the mayor's engagements for coming week or called in at the town hall.

No signing-in was then necessary. No visitor's badge. You just nodded to Rita Leach at her cats-cradle switchboard and sauntered upstairs to the town clerk's department for a leisurely natter with Ann and her colleagues.

Sometimes the blindingly obvious is denied you until the veil is lifted from your eyes. I realised, belatedly, how much I enjoyed these visits - "liaison calls" Tony Tubb had called them when chief reporter. Analysing why the visits were so much fun, I realised that it was Ann's friendly, cheery personality.

Plucking up courage, I asked what she was doing on Friday night.

"Playing badminton."

Trounced.

I tried again another week. She had her answer ready: "Washing my hair."

This gal was playing hard to get and I was becoming more determined. I was also becoming a little desperate. I had a feeling that I was suffering the onset of something rather more than friendship.

A couple more polite rebuttals and I would be becoming a pest and risk losing everything.

Tony Tubb had invited me to one of his house-warmings. He was moving on a regular basis at that time because speculative house-building was decidedly more profitable than journalism.

I adopted a more calculated approach with Ann the following Friday.

"I suppose you are playing badminton tonight...."

Yes.

"That means you will be washing your hair tomorrow night…"

The smile told me she knew I was up to something but was not sure what.

Yes.

"Right - Tony has invited me to bring a friend to a house-warming party on Sunday night. That must mean that you are free."

We owe what at the time of writing is 40 years of happiness together to the fact that Ann is too nice a girl to tell a boy to get lost in as many words.

Instead, seizing her escape route, she phoned me at home on the Sunday morning to announce (a little too delightedly for my liking) that it was snowing. As I had just changed my car she fully appreciated that I would not want to drive my new pride and joy (a £300 third-hand Hillman Minx) to Little Common that evening.

I stuck to my guns and said that if necessary we could catch a bus. I walked from Church Vale Road to Suffolk Road in near-blizzard conditions. We found the buses weren't running. So we set out to walk the two miles to Little Common. It was cold but we had plenty to chat about. Our fathers both worked for SEGAS.

"My dad knows your dad ..." later became our catch-phrase, recalling that night.

Such were the conditions, that Ann and I were Tony and Denise's *only* guests. Naturally, there were lashings of food. After a lovely evening, we set out to walk home - snowballing each other as we went.

At the corner of Suffolk Road and Sidley Street I chanced my luck with a chaste good-night kiss. My sense of humour will be my undoing one day. I risked losing everything when I put my arms around her by saying "Long way round isn't it…?" (She was wearing a thick winter coat).

Fortunately, Ann also has a good sense of humour. Somehow, both of us sensed that the next time I asked her out a way would be found round the badminton / hair-wash impasse.

Bill Sansom was to become the last Mayor that Ann served as secretary. She had helped Bill set up a local committee of what was then Action Research for the Crippled Child before leaving to have our son, Paul.

We nearly lost Paul when he was a month old. He still bears the scar of an operation from which he developed complications. In gratitude for his recovery, Ann became branch secretary for Action Research, a voluntary post which she held for many years.

Bill and his wife, Doreen, became two of Paul's Godparents.

5 How do you spell that, please?

RAIN was running down my neck. London Road was grey and dank. I was standing on the steps of St John's Church, in the early '60s still a Congregational establishment before the advent of the United Reformed Church.

"Your name please, sir?"

I was on the junior reporters' least favourite assignment - taking the names of those attending the funeral of some town worthy. We still maintained the old practice then and woe betide any reporter who got a name wrong, especially if the possessor was a friend of the Old Man's.

It was tedious. It was time-consuming and it was stultifyingly boring. The tall, distinguished gentleman gave me his name courteously. Notebook fast becoming as sodden as its user, I duly wrote down "A.J.R. Scott".

"No," he said, repeating his name. I looked at my note and asked him to repeat again. Again, I wrote it down as heard. He shook his head. We were getting nowhere.

Silently, he took my notebook and pen. "A.J. Arscott" he wrote - and all became clear.

It was my first introduction to Jethro Arscott, later to become not only a good contact, but a valued friend and mentor.

Really, I had no excuse for not knowing his name. My late Aunt Annie had been his nursemaid in far-off pre-war days when such ladies were commonplace in better-off homes in the town.

Little did I realise that, four decades on, I would be following in more modest form in Jethro's footsteps in one respect.

One of the little talks I give to organisations in the town concerns the campaign which led to the building - entirely by voluntary fund-raising - of Bexhill Hospital.

It was opened in 1933 entirely free of debt - a remarkable achievement in a post-Depression era.

By 1952 when the shock of "losing" this independent local asset with the creation of National Health Service in 1948 had faded, a new body was formed which was very much in the spirit of that founding appeal body.

One of the founding fathers' of Bexhill Hospital was Jethro Arscott (senior). The committee's early meetings were held in the family bakery and confectionary business in St Leonards Road.

One of the founders of the League of Friends of Bexhill Hospital was his son, also Jethro, a prominent local solicitor and later head of his practice.

It was Jethro (junior) who suggested to the editor that what the League needed was a higher public profile. Would the editor care to serve on its committee?

Instead, The Old Man "volunteered" me. Jethro jumped at the opportunity, welcoming me to the table with the words that such a "young man" (this is a very old story) would undoubtedly outlive the rest of them and serve the league well.

That first meeting was, to the best of my recollection, in 1966. I did as was bid. I reported for the Observer on the league's work until my retirement and at the time of writing this have every intention of continuing to contribute stories about the league's work for as long as either organisation wants me to do.

Jethro served the league with distinction until his death. He was a dedicated and charismatic chairman and continued his good work as president.

His enduring contribution to the League's work was to suggest (in his winning manner) to clients when drafting their wills that rather than let the Chancellor of the Exchequer snatch their money they might care to leave it to the league of friends.

In this he was continuing to draw on the same fund of goodwill in the town which had brought such success to his father's campaign, with its long-remembered "Buy a Brick" scheme.

It was his influence and the work of generations of faithful league volunteers who followed that enabled the League to make such major investments in the work of Bexhill Hospital as its £1.175 million refurbishment which helped the Irvine Unit there to match 21st Century needs.

I could not have imagined as I stood outside St John's in the rain all those years ago that I would be writing this as league president. But as Ann always says, she "married into" the League of Friends in 1969.

As part of another long-lasting friendship, she was secretary to Bill Sansom when he was organiser of the league's annual garden party. When Bill died and the league could not find a successor she took on both roles, fulfilling them for many years until the pressure of caring for her aged mother forced her to quit.

She continues as league committee member and at time of writing is poised to take over as league secretary to relieve Peter Mitchell-Davis who became acting secretary after five years as chairman.

It's *that* sort of organisation. "Once bitten…"

6 Generous to a fault

NOBODY who has spent even the briefest time working on a local paper should be under any illusion about provincial newspaper groups' capacity for parsimony. We three learnt some hard lessons in double-quick time.

We started our careers in what was a hastily-converted former garage. The offices of the Bexhill Observer were in Devonshire Road until May 9, 1942 – the anniversary of the paper's founding in 1896 – when Adolf Hitler bestowed a birthday present, delivered by the Luftwaffe.

The offices were destroyed, hence our beginnings in the early '60s in Western Road. The '60s they surely were. "Swinging" they definitely were not in those conditions.

Beneath us was the customary fusty front office. Behind and beneath us was F.J. Parsons Ltd's print works. Some of the readership entering the front office and hearing the clattering letterpress behind imagined the Observer was printed there.

It wasn't and never had been. It was printed at Parsons' Cambridge Road works in Hastings – but thereby hangs another tale for us.

The Bexhill editorial offices were accessed by a wide, shallow staircase ending on a landing with an unedifying vista over the corrugated roof of the works.

The offices, like the rest of the building, were of uniform shabbiness. Four reporters sat round a cluster of ancient desks. The sub-editor inhabited a desk on his own by the door. Later, a doorway way knocked through a wall, allowed a store room (with no direct natural light) to accommodate two other reporters.

The editor's office had a door directly from the corridor and another from the reporters' room.

On the other side of the reporters' room lay kitchen-cum-staffroom with a grubby sink and an ancient cooker.

Precipitous back-stairs led down to the works. The gents' toilets were a day's march away from editorial – through the kitchen, down the stairs, across the works and into an area which had its origins in the former Bijou Cinema.

Casting an eye up from one's concentration on the job in hand in the urinal, one could still discern the decorative plaster coving which once graced the Bijou.

Jimmy Burke, the Observer's skilled but famously irascible photographer, inhabited a darkroom which was still further distant – across the print room, through the composing room where type was still set by hand and up a flight of wooden stairs into the roof.

There, poor Jimmy alternately sweated or froze according to season over his reeking tanks of developer and print chemicals and the enlarger which was the source of much of his near-magical skills.

The question of office temperature was always a vexed one. If the Old Man ruled editorial with a rod of iron, the works manager, Roland "Rowie" Reeve, was God reigning over his preserve from his ground floor office.

This applied in particular to the question of when the central heating was switched on and off.

This bore no relation to weather conditions but solely to the calendar. Rowie Reeve was inflexible on the issue – until a feisty school-leaver by the name of Gill Marsh had the temerity to contest the point.

Fed up with sitting shivering in the draughty office with its linoleum floor, Gill phoned the town hall and invoked the Offices, Shops and Railway Premises Act. The office was below the prescribed temperature and the works manager found himself obliged to spend company money on heating its workers well ahead of his self-imposed date.

He was not pleased. In fact he was fuming. But there was nothing he could do.

That lino was well past its sell-by date long before We Three arrived. It had rippled as it stretched and rose off the concrete floor. The ripples became bubbles and, in time, the bubbles burst.

Torn lino would be unthinkable in this health and safety-obsessed age. Then, we were simply told when we complained that it was a trip-risk to "pick your feet up..."

Eventually, I decided that Gill's approach was the right one.

The worst rip was behind my desk. It was on a major thoroughfare, strategically placed along Rowie Reeve's route from his office to the Old Man's. Omitting to "pick my feet up," I contrived to put my foot in it and judiciously extend the rip.

Rowie ascended the stairs at his usual pace and strode through our office on route to the editor's. The crash as he tripped over the rip and spread his length on the floor was joy to our adolescent ears.

Nothing was said. But the lino was swiftly replaced with new-fangled vinyl.

Motor scooters soon dropped us in deepest doo-doo. Only editors and works managers got to see the inside of the F.J. Parsons Ltd. board room at Cambridge Road, Hastings. So, when John Liddle and I received an imperious summons from "FJ" to explain our expenses claims we were filled with foreboding.

The board room was a region of distressed grandeur in that grimy building but it could have been Buckingham Palace to us.

A tentative tap at the door brought a grunt from within. We timorous two walked the length of the room to stand in front of a massive desk resplendent with ancient two-piece telephone.

Eventually, and not having offered us a seat. "FJ" began to grill us. What did we mean by these "extravagant" expenses claims? What was the mileage for? Very well then, who *asked* us to use these ... er ... motor scooters. The term was evidently not one with which the owner of a massive Bentley and who lived in a country seat approached by a lengthy drive, was conversant.

The tone of the interrogation became more terse. It was all or nothing. I again opted for the Marsh approach. Nobody had asked us to use these, er, motor scooters. It had been our own idea – and at our own personal expense.

But why did we use them for the firm's business? Did we not have the use of our legs…?

I explained that I was blessed with a good pair of legs, that my hobby was rambling in the country, that I would be delighted to walk from assignment to assignment, interview to interview.

I was rewarded with the ghost of a smile as the thought of saving money – petrol then cost 4s. 6d. (22.5p) a gallon and "Cleo" would happily run for a week on less than this – crossed his mind.

"But it would mean that you would get less work done because it would take me half the day to get out to Little Common and back …"

The smile faded. We were dismissed with a weary wave of the hand. The "extravagant" expenses claims continued.

7 Adding fuel to the flames

RULE No 1 when covering fires is "Don't hinder the firefighters." They were still called firemen when I turned out to one of my first blazes as a junior reporter. I was mindful of the golden rule but, sadly, my first attempts at carrying it out produced mixed results.

The fire siren had still to be supplanted by the personal alerter in the early '60s. Twice in a row one winter's morning the siren disturbed the (relative) peace of the Western Road office. Twice I rang the old Amherst Road fire station only to be told that they were off on a chimney fire. Then as now, these rated a NIB (News In Brief paragraph) at the most.

The third time the siren went I was all for ignoring it. "Better check, lad - you never know, this could be the big one."

The Voice of Experience was Jimmy Burke's. As usual, he was right. It had been snowing hard. When we got to the end of the long, private drive, the elderly householder was sitting forlornly on a sofa salvaged from the flames and watching her beloved home burn.

Contrasted against the snow, the dark smoke looked even more ominous. Just as we arrived, flames burst through the roof.

Even I knew that when a fire gets to that stage it is serious. The firemen were going to need all their skill plus a good deal of luck if they were to save much of the semi-bungalow from destruction.

The two Bexhill machines were already in action. We could hear the bell (this is a '60s story, remember) as reinforcements arrived in another appliance from neighbouring Hastings.

Jimmy was hard at work with his museum-piece VN half-plate camera.

"Move that ruddy van NOW!"

The van was blocking the narrow access road. The firemen's Assistant Divisional Officer was in no mood for delay.

"I'll do it..." rashly offered this school-leaver, neglecting to add that he had never driven anything with four wheels.

Without taking his eye from the view-finder, Jimmy tossed me the key to the Bexhill Observer's sole means of staff transport - a much-abused Mini-Van.

Crunch! I got the van into first gear. Mindful of the need not to stall it and make a fool of myself, I trod heavily on the accelerator.

The van lurched forward about two feet, ran over the hosepipe and burst it before stalling. With the Mini in a mini-fountain I floundered, found reverse, buried the accelerator and shot backwards.

Well, how was I to know the firemen had laid a second hose behind the van..?

Eventually, amid many kind and encouraging remarks from my firemen "contacts" (none of which would bear repetition here) I got the offending vehicle out of the way without further damage.

Later, with the fire under control and in an act of contrition which would certainly not be permissible in today's health and safety-conscious age, I went into the ruins and helped salvage further household treasures for the poor soul sitting on the sofa in the snow.

A pair of old-fashioned kitchen scales come in so handy when one has been made homeless by a combination of misfortune and a junior reporter's clumsiness...

In retrospect, I feel privileged to have spent my early working life in a pre-health and safety age.

Safer it may be today, but life is so much more constrained. It is certainly a lot less fun.

In the era when Cleo, my trusty motor scooter, was still my hack, I got a tip-off at home one foggy evening.

Peering into the murk, I set forth. As I made my way as fast as I dared along West Parade a police officer stepped out of the gloom.

"What's the hurry, sonny? Wanna get yourself killed?" Then, recognising me, "Oh, hello, John. Well, what *is* the hurry?"

He soon saw the need for expedition when I told him a bomb had been found on the beach. He cocked a leg over the pannier bags and rode pillion to the far end of the prom.

A Royal Naval ordnance disposal team was coming up the beach bearing a mortar bomb.

"Where can we blow this where it won't do any damage?"

I suggested the beach at Herbrand Walk. It was a couple of miles away and the far end was several hundred yards from the nearest house.

But how to guide them there in the fog?

Eventually, it was agreed that I should ride in their vehicle - *with* the bomb.

It was doubtless a "dud," they assured me. Probably that's why it had been abandoned. We drove along South Cliff, scene of a school of trench warfare in the Great War, long before the area was developed with some of the town's most desirable and high-priced homes, and the source of many finds of the "unexploded" variety.

Herbrand Walk was, as expected, deserted on such a night. It was low tide. I was allowed to carry the bomb down to the beach. The team strapped plastic explosive and a detonator to it, covered it with sand-bags and we withdrew.

"If it goes off with white smoke it was a dud. If the smoke is black it was live," they explained.

Just in case it was live we sheltered behind a groyne and they gave me a spare helmet.

"Get down and stay down after it goes."

I did as I was told. I can still hear the patter of the falling debris on that helmet now as that "dud" went off.

What's round and flat and found on beaches like ours? Given the fact that Bexhill is plainly marked as a landing zone on Nazi documents planning Operation Sealion, the invasion of Great Britain, anti-tank mines were a distinct possibility.

It was thus that with commendable courage that PC Mike Dean, our town centre copper, approached a round and flat object at the water's edge - again at West Parade.

He was worried. It was below high water mark so the Royal Navy had been called but it would take them until well after the next tide had come in to reach Bexhill from Portsmouth.

By that time the suspect device would have been washed back out to sea.

"Why not borrow a dan buoy from one of the fishing boats and tie that to it?" a helpful Dowling suggested.

To his credit, Mike did not hesitate. The Observer's picture showed him advancing with caution, buoy and rope in hand.

The Navy team commended him after they arrived. The device had not been washed far by the tide and the buoy marked the spot.

But, story-wise, there was a disappointment. This was no anti-invasion device when they got to it but the concrete base of one of those old temporary bus stops.

We decided to turn the situation to advantage. We ran the story - plus the picture - with a "Brave PC Dean and the unexploded bus stop" heading.

He waited a while before he got his revenge.

It was my habit to get into the office early. But it was no ordinary morning a few weeks later when we had all forgotten the unexploded bus stop. I pulled out my chair to sit down. A file "jumped" off the shelf with a clatter. I moved my typewriter. My in-tray followed it.

"Gotcha!" Mike emerged grinning from behind the door.

I happily agreed to his request not to spoil the surprise for chief reporter Deb Scott-Bromley and the others.

When Mike had gone into Rene's, the town's fishing tackle shop, and asked for some fishing line, to determine what breaking strain this non-angler needed they had asked what he wanted to catch.

"Those rotters at the Observer!" Mike told them.

When I was a schoolboy, the Chantry Community Primary School building in Barrack Road was still called St Peter's Church of England Infant and Junior School.

"There's Army Land Rovers outside Chantry with red-painted front wings," said the good-hearted soul who phoned the office with a tip-off in 1989.

That could mean only one thing - a bomb disposal unit was in town. A photographer and I shot off for Barrack Road.

The school had been evacuated by the time we arrived. We explained to the squaddie guarding the gate who we were and asked if he could let the officer in charge know that we would be grateful for a picture and a comment when his dangerous work was done. Eventually the officer emerged.

"Know what this is?" he asked me.

"World War Two German incendiary," I replied with more confidence than I felt, adding: "De-activated."

Somewhat non-plussed, he said I was well-informed. I then had to make a confession.

Beside the school there still stood at that stage the former Barrack Road Police Station, little bigger than a detached Victorian house but with its own cell with bijou barred window.

It was used as a school office by 1989 but when I was at Senior School my pal Bryan Graves lived there - his dad was a sergeant.

I was the proud possessor of a bayonet, two English army helmets and one German helmet. We were well-served for boyish games of soldiers for Bryan owned an American army helmet and ... er ... a Second World War German incendiary bomb (de-activated).

"I suppose you found it stuffed under the rafters in the cell?"

That was where Bryan kept his bike in the old days - and his bomb.

"Sorry about the evacuation and all that ..."

The Sackville Hotel was the jewel in the town's crown. For years after The Sackville's conversion into flats, the mantle fell on the next largest establishment, The Granville in Sea Road.

The Granville evolved by sale into The Grand in its latter days. But it was long-vacant and the haunt both of squatters and of fire-setting vandals when it met its sad demise.

My wife and I had been to a dinner. Following our usual practice, she being far more abstemious than me, she had driven home. We had just got the gates open when we heard two-tones as fire engines raced into Bexhill from Hastings.

This was something serious. And I couldn't drive. Without a word Ann, bless her, got back behind the wheel. There was no question where the fire was. The Grand was like a huge beacon in the night as we re-entered town. I left Ann sitting in the dark as I ran along Jameson Road.

True The Grand had seen better days. True it was empty and unlikely to re-open as a hotel. But, like so many other townspeople, I had spent so many happy hours there. The dining room and ballroom had been the scene of so many dinner-dances. Like the hotel, these were things of the past - the Tradesmen's Ball, the Independent Schools Association annual dinners and, most significantly of all, the late-lamented Hotels Association.

Now the grand old lady was being consumed on her own funeral pyre, slowly and sadly collapsing inwards as greedy flames devoured her.

It was a busy night. Get hold of a photographer on the phone; interview folk who had been evacuated from their homes; the vicar who had given them refuge in his church hall;

Matt Dargan the licensee who had brought welcome cups of tea to the firefighters and, lastly, when at last he was free, the fire chief.

I had arrived some time after ten. My watch now said gone 2am.

Ann! I ran back to the car where a white-faced wife waited in cross-legged desperation. There are no public loos open in Bexhill at that hour and it had been a long time since that dinner...

The story was a big one. It was, of course, arson. The follow-up story concerned the joint police-fire service investigation. Imagine the amusement of friends and "contacts" in both police and fire station when our chief photographer in Hastings, Justin Lycett, e-mailed me just one extra picture.

In front of the blazing building had been superimposed a crouching figure holding a can of petrol. My face had been put on the body.

The Grand Hotel arsonist is seen running from the scene in this spoof picture nailing the bearded culprit. Top right: The Old Man, himself, our first editor Len Bartley with his wife, Edith. Below: JD needs all the help he can get with new technology and students from St Mary's School, Wrestwood, are happy to oblige on an office visit.

Renowned Bexhill Observer photographer Jimmy Burke. Right, his picture of a helmeted John Dowling preparing a first-hand account of a fire at Pebsham Farm. Below, young Dowling gets a chuckle from Malcolm Muggeridge at a Rotary Club public speaking contest.

Under Penland Wood, young Dowling goes where others fear to tread. Right: the Bexhill Observer offices in Western Road, where it all started for John, Ken and Philip in the '60s. Below: one of the many dramatic stories covered by John, the fire at Cooden Beach Hotel.

8 Weathering the Storm

WHERE news-gathering is concerned there is no happy medium. People who ask "Are you busy?" always get the same reply: "If there's news about, we're busy. If there's no news about we are busy trying to find some."

There was certainly no lack of news copy that memorable morning in October 1987.

I missed Michael Fish's oft-repeated television denial the night before that a hurricane was coming Britain's way. I was out and there was certainly nothing to indicate that trouble was brewing.

But brew it did. The storm broke with fearsome suddenness just as Ann and I got to bed. It was the only occasion on which my wife absolutely forbade me going out on the Observer's service. She was right. Slates, tiles, tree branches and shards of glass were flying in a lethal maelstrom.

We had just had double-glazing installed. The salesman said it would be completely draught-proof. He didn't specify whether it would resist conditions which later became known as The Great Storm.

We'd heard the wind get up. The electricity failed when power lines all across the South East came down. We lay in bed in total darkness listening to the wind *shrieking* through the "draught-proof" double-glazing.

Above the din, we could hear an inexplicable scraping noise out in the road. When dawn finally broke we discovered it was a large tree being blown lengthways down the road.

My father was 82. He had suffered with a severe heart condition since he was 60 (he lived to be 100!). My first thought when dawn broke was to check that he and his bungalow were unhurt.

Then to get working. But where? And how? I made contact with the redoubtable Jimmy Burke and together we set about what was to be a hopeless task. Stories and pictures abounded. There was no chance of covering them all.

Instead, with the help of the rest of Observer team we cherry-picked the best. The Sackville Road office had lost its roof. But, miraculously, the phones still worked.

The MP was less fortunate. His constituency office was cut off. He made our Editorial office his temporary headquarters as he tried to get an overview of the situation.

Flats in Hastings Road were among the worst-hit. Jimmy got pictures of St John Ambulance volunteers wheeling bewildered elderly residents to temporary shelter.

Debris littered every street. Crunching through the broken glass and tiles, I spotted an odd sight in South Cliff. Something large and flat with spikes sticking out of it lay in the road.

It was the entire covering of what had been a flat-roofed house. I looked for a house with no roof and knocked the door. The householder seemed somewhat relieved to see a figure in wellie boots, over-trousers, reflective jacket and builder's safety helmet on his doorstep.

His belief that help had come was quickly dashed when I announced myself. With great courtesy, he led me up an elegant staircase to the top corridor. With a flourish, he flung open a door.

"*That* was my bedroom," he said sadly. It was open above to the still-malevolent sky. Where the rear wall and window would have been was a panorama of raging sea at the foot of the low cliff. Thankfully, Bexhill suffered no fatalities.

The luckiest man in town was the owner of a West Parade penthouse. Neighbours in the flats below had just managed finally to persuade him to evacuate his eerie when the whole structure was blown off the top of the block. It crashed onto the garage block below.

And the Dunkirk spirit was not far away. At Cooden Sea Road I found a group of neighbours beavering away with chainsaws at a tangled mass of fallen trees which were blocking the road.

Most roads were impassable because of such obstructions. Realising that it would be days before county highways and their contractors to get to many areas, they had taken matters into their own hands.

I doubt if any of them was less than 70. They were having the time of their lives.

Northeye prison officer Barry Wilkinson's pride and joy was the weather station he had constructed at the jail. It was an invaluable educational tool for the inmates.

But it was Barry who, at the height of the storm, had stepped outside and, bracing himself against the tempest sweeping in from the exposed Pevensey Marsh, had held an anemometer aloft long enough to get a wind-speed reading. It was 98mph.

Eventually, it was time to return to the roofless office and get to work. Jimmy disappeared into his dark room to begin developing and printing countless rolls of 35mm film – all monochrome in those days.

When eventually he emerged, one of his unforgettable gems was a shot of a boat which the wind had left "beached" outside a shop half-way up Sackville Road – about 300 yards from the seafront!

So many stories; so many pictures; so many angles to cover and follow-ups to undertake. That week's paper was practically a one-subject issue. The front page picture and story told of a mother's frantic dash to get through the blocked streets at the height of the storm and reach hospital before her baby was born.

But even this couldn't do justice to what had happened. There was only one answer – a special edition. But I'll leave Philip Elms to tell how his "baby" was delivered.

9 Breaking the news

BREAKING the news does not always mean telling the readers first. On one memorable occasion it was necessary first to tell the individual concerned that he was about to become the centre of one of the biggest news stories to hit Bexhill.

Nicholas Walsh was the man chosen to be chief executive when Rother District Council was set up in 1974.

He didn't last long. By 1978 critics within the council were lining up against him. I knew from contacts within the council that the matter was becoming increasingly serious. Then one morning I got a tip-off that led me to make an unaccustomedly early knock on a councillor's door.

I wanted to catch Doug Haynes before he left home. I wanted to confirm a story. It was one that would not only give the Observer an exclusive front page that week but which would keep, the local paper, the nationals and the specialist local government journals in copy for weeks.

Doug was surprised to see me at such an hour. He was even more surprised when I asked him to confirm that he was planning to propose that Rother make its own chief executive and his assistant redundant.

He didn't want to comment. He was about to shut the door when I explained that I had chapter-and-verse on the movement to oust the chief, would value his comment and contribution but would be duty-bound to write the story whether he gave his side or not.

He invited me in and told me all.

Nicholas Walsh was out of the office when I called. I tried later. It was on the very eve of going to press. He was aghast. He had no idea that matters had come to such a head.

It was not a pleasant interview to undertake. I had got on well with him and liked him.

It was this issue which led to my covering the longest-ever Rother Council meeting. Naturally, council went into secret session to discuss its reasons for wanting to make its own chief and his assistant redundant. I sat out the agonisingly long period with the chief in his office.

Conversation did not come easily as he awaited the verdict.

Mr Walsh, a solicitor, took Rother to an industrial tribunal for unfair dismissal, which I covered.

He later went on to a distinguished legal career. Rother on the other hand went through a troubled period. Having made their chief and his assistant redundant, councillors could not then in law replace him.

Instead, a triumvirate of officers was appointed to run the show. It didn't work and after an interval the council reverted to having a sole post-holder at the helm.

But those were the days when the Observer had a team of six reporters, twice what it had when I left. Although e-mail and the like did not exist to make sending news copy to national papers the simple matter it is now, we had time then to do linage - in which freelance news stories are paid for by the line. Nick Walsh's departure from the town hall eased the pain of our monthly home mortgage for a while.

A local reporter who acts for a national paper or news agency in a town is known as a stringer. Our team were stringers for anyone who would pay us linage. The company rule was that one could sell a story provided it did not prejudice the paper's interests.

The current convention that we would be giving away to all and sundry virtually every story we got as soon as we got it would have been unthinkable. It was instant dismissal if by a loose tongue you lost the Observer an exclusive.

What would that generation of editors have made of today's websites, where papers give readers for free what previously provide cover-charge income and much-coveted circulation?

Being a stringer nearly dropped me in very hot water indeed. One of the great journalistic challenges was (and still is) to be first with each General Election result.

BBC and ITV pay stringers to telephone them figures as each poll in a General Election is announced. There is a useful bonus for beating anyone else who is acting for a rival.

Today, David Millward is transport correspondent of the Daily Telegraph. He began his training with the Bexhill Observer. He was known as Ace in the Observer office because he (and we) always knew he would make it to the top.

We were then still a Saturday paper (the Observer is published on Friday now). General Elections are traditionally held on a Thursday. This was semi-convenient. It meant that if all went well the Observer could carry Thursday's result on Saturday.

But it depended on all going to plan. And on one occasion it didn't. It went wrong - very wrong. General Elections never make exciting news in Bexhill, where the Tory vote is usually overwhelming. On this occasion tired election staff were devastated by a call for a re-count. Who would be going to Westminster was not in dispute. It was who would lose their deposit.

Back Dave and I trooped the following morning, still jaded like the election staff as they set to work on the re-count. At the print works at Hastings fingers were being gnawed as the clock ticked to deadline.

Horrors! Another who's-come-last argument led to a *second* re-count. Now the Observer really was in deep trouble. Our deadline had been extended. But the paper could not be held indefinitely.

The count was being held in Bexhill Amateur Athletic Club's sports centre. Mobile phones were still a thing of the future. There was one pay-phone. I sent Dave to occupy the booth with instructions to make a transfer-charge call to the Hastings office and hold the line no matter who came pounding on the door.

The weary counters worked with agonising slowness, conscious that the candidates' agents were watching carefully. Eventually, a declaration of poll drew near.

At this stage, the Agents always confer with the returning officer to agree on spoilt papers and other matters. The discussion dragged on...

Eventually, I could wait no longer and, peeking over Rother chief executive David Powell's shoulder, made a mental note of the poll figures. I ran to the phone with a scribbled note for Dave. He did his duty and passed the message to the office.

Job done! And done well.

Er ... job done *too* well. Dave also dutifully phoned P.A. (Press Association), for whom we were stringing and whose bonus cheque for being first with the result we eagerly awaited.

Alongside the gym at the BAAC sports centre and with a window between the two is the club's bar. In the bar a group representing all the political parties was eagerly following the national television coverage.

David Powell stood in the gym with the Bexhill and Rye Constituency result in his hand. "I being the returning officer..." he began to intone.

But his announcement was drowned by the cheering from the bar as the BBC broadcast the election result. The chief executive turned to me: "How did that happen, John ...?"

The Gallic shrug had to suffice.

10 Over the wire

WITH the laudable Christian exception of Bexhill Council of Churches, every town organisation – including the Observer – thought the idea of a jail in town spelled disaster with a capital D.

The Home Office Prison Department certainly couldn't ignore a vacant former RAF camp as a potential new prison site.

Back in 1966, prison overcrowding was becoming a national crisis. Emergency measures were called for and the Mountbatten Report recommended making use of such former military bases. The Observer campaigned vigorously. Protest meetings were held by town organisations. Inevitably, the issue went to an Inquiry, which I covered.

But despite the vehement protestations of impending doom expressed at the inquiry, the result was a foregone conclusion.

The Home Office put a 17ft wire fence round the billets, mess hall, administration block, chapel and sick bay of the former RAF Wartling and a 12ft fence round the sports field and called it HMP Northeye. It really was as crude as that.

Northeye was designated as a Category C prison, Category A being top-security and Category D open prisons.

Category C prisoners were defined as those presenting little or no risk to the community but lacking the willpower to escape from totally open conditions.

Prisoners were accommodated in the billets – hastily thrown up by the War Department when Wartling was built as a war-time radar station. The billets could not be locked at night because of the fire risk and in any case were not secure. The only thing preventing 250 inmates from walking away from Northeye was the fence.

The inquiry was assured that Royal Marine commandos had been set the task of scaling such a fence and had failed. The first escapee went over the wire within a short time of Northeye opening. So much for inquiry assurances.

Such was the novelty of the situation that Jimmy Burke and I spent half a night chasing police and prison officers as they scoured Pevensey Marsh for the first escapee.

The novelty didn't last long. Escapes became so commonplace that their news value diminished rapidly to a couple of paragraphs. But, despite governor Larry Stones inviting the public to visit Northeye, meet the staff and inmates and see what life was like on the inside, the legacy of town hostility to Northeye persisted.

It was against this background that I received an unexpected request. Larry phoned and asked if I knew what a prison Board of Visitors was – and would I join Northeye's board?

Board members are Home Office appointees; people drawn from all walks of life in the local community charged with ensuring that the State treats prisoners according to the law.

On production of their identity card, board members can demand entrance to their appointed establishment at any time, day or night, inspect any section of the prison, see any prisoner in private – and sample the food. Boards make annual reports to the Home Office. They have a quasi-judicial role, tribunals conducting disciplinary hearings where prisoners are accused of offences beyond the punitive powers of the governor.

I told Larry Stones it wouldn't work. There would be a conflict of interest. I would want to write news stories for the Observer about what I saw and heard in Northeye – and he would want to hush up what I had found.

He was persistent. Phone calls followed the same pattern until one day Larry played his trump card.

"There's a new Home Office directive. 'Where possible, try and recruit your local newspaper editor…'

It could have added "Or deputy editor…" I was cornered. My Northeye "sentence" was to last 13 years until the prison was closed in 1992.

Membership was to take me to meetings at the Home Office, to lunch at Northeye with Home Secretary Douglas Hurd, to the biggest story I ever handled – and to some of the most hair-raising *and* humorous situations in my life.

Northeye's inmates were not exactly big-time professional criminals, though in its latter years and, again, in contradiction of assurances given at the inquiry, prisoners with convictions for sex and violence were sent to Bexhill in their final months before release.

Rather, most were life's losers – petty criminals, recidivists, embezzlers and "mules" duped by traffickers into carrying drugs into the country.

Consequently, though many escaped, this was a reflection of the low level of security rather than the ingenuity and resource of the individual. In short, some were not very bright.

In the early years, one of the products turned out in Northeye's workshop was plastic-covered wire display racks for Sunblest bread. The brighter workshop inmates quickly crafted hand-held wire hooks together with spikes to drive into the toes of their boots and simply clambered over the fence at night.

Some tried other dodges.

One individual went round his billet one stormy night – and Northeye must be one of the most bleak and exposed spots in the district - while his colleagues were at "association time" watching television he pinched the mattresses off their beds.

He piled a pyramid of bedding against the wire and carefully put a mattress protectively over the barbed wire at the top before cocking a leg over. Freedom beckoned until a particularly stormy gust blew him off his precarious perch.

Guess on which side of the fence he landed?

My favourite episode was the enterprising individual who, having obviously seen Colditz and other prisoner-of-war films, reasoned that a flat-bed lorry with a convenient tarpaulin which made regular deliveries at Northeye offered a ticket to freedom.

He seized his opportunity. He hid under the tarpaulin and, having not been detected when the lorry was stopped at the gate, calculated that after three quarters of an hour or so he would be

30 miles or more from captivity and could slip over the tailboard when the lorry stopped. The lorry stopped. He slipped over the tailboard – and found himself in Lewes Prison yard!

Danny Ozanne had the misfortune to be governor at a troubled time. He rang me at home one Sunday morning. There was a problem. He needed a board of visitors member in a hurry.

I found Danny and the chief officer backed up against the gate leading from the main compound to the sports field.

In front of them bayed a large and angry crowd of Nigerian prisoners – mainly convicted hapless drug mules.

"Here comes the board of visitors member now," Danny bellowed over the din. All eyes turned on yours truly. Clearly, I was expected to perform some miracle of conciliation.

An inmate who had been a member of the Nigerian national football team had languished on remand in "The Scrubs." He had been sent to Northeye on conviction and had thrown himself with abandon into the task at Northeye's magnificent sports hall of getting himself fit once again.

Alas, he was not as fit as he had imagined. During an energetic soccer match he collapsed and died.

His pals' anger was symptomatic of the cultural divide. Coming from a hot country, the Nigerians were accustomed to swift action in such circumstances – not the protracted English practice of keeping the deceased on the soccer field until the prison doctor could be located and brought from his home some miles away to pronounce their pal dead.

Eventually, Danny and I persuaded the mob to elect two spokesmen to discuss the situation more soberly in Danny's office. We managed to explain that no disrespect to the dead was implied by leaving him on the field. He would be taken to the prison chapel as soon as the formalities were over.

There still remained the difficulty of getting a response from the Nigerian Embassy in London and so getting word to the dead man's family back home.

Danny tried but got the "It's Sunday. There's nobody here" treatment from a bored Embassy factotum.

"May I try?" asked one of the spokesmen. There followed a rapid-fire and somewhat spirited phone call that Danny and I could not, of course, understand. All was sorted.

"How did you do that?"

"Sir, I am a tribal chief. I told the man to pull his finger out…"

Fires were a not uncommon occurrence at Northeye. A little arson now and again was a means of expression. I spent most of one Boxing Day watching disgruntled prisoners stone a fire engine which had come under attack while responding to a blaze.

The clothing store seemed to be the principal victim of such attacks. The usual dodge was to lob a lighted toilet roll into the store and watch the newly-laundered uniforms go up in smoke.

The last words I said to my wife as I set off in response to a call to a fire one evening in April 1986 were: "It's probably the clothing store again. I'll be back by about 7.30…"

It was 7.30 – but 7.30 the following morning!

I was heading for Northeye with, as usual, two responsibilities – one to the BoV and the other to the Bexhill Observer.

I should have realised that Northeye was heading for the big showdown. The Home Office had increased Northeye's registered roll – its maximum inmate population - but without corresponding increases in staffing and security. Past experience showed that this was asking for trouble.

The board in its annual report at the start of the year had warned in blunt terms that the internal pressure this move had made could lead to "riot or even death".

From Bexhill's only stretch of dual-carriageway, King Offa Way, there is a hill-top view over the western side of town. Northeye lay over the horizon about four miles distant.

As I topped the rise I could see a pall of smoke like something from the set of a war film. The problem was going to be bigger than just the clothing store.

The scene which greeted me at Northeye was nightmarish. Fires were raging in a dozen different buildings. Prisoners with stocking masks were systematically smashing windows. Any prison officer who showed himself was pelted with potatoes with razor blades inserted in them.

I was met by Danny at the main gate. I was the only board member available. With no great conviction I asked if he wanted me to go and try and talk to the rioters.

Every prison has an agreed emergency plan. Danny swiftly reminded me of Northeye's. Because of its nature, Northeye could only operate with a degree of inmate cooperation. In the event of a serious riot there was no chance of holding the situation.

And this was a major riot. In such circumstances, the worse thing that could happen was for the rioters to obtain a hostage – and therefore absolute power. I was off the hook. But Northeye was in deep trouble.

All the prison officers had successfully made their safe exit. The first stage of the emergency plan was therefore accomplished. The second stage was now underway – to hold the perimeter and prevent a mass escape by the inmates.

This was no easy matter as Northeye was a large, scattered site on the edge of town and bordered for the most part by open fields. I had set out with nothing warmer than a sports jacket. The April night was chill but it was to be warm work.

The Bexhill riot was part of an orchestrated plan of unrest throughout the national prison system. The first thing the rioters had done was to wreck the administration block and put the phones out of action.

The former RAF Married Quarters outside the wire housed prison officers and their families. It was from there that Danny and his team communicated with an increasingly overwhelmed Home Office Prison Department and with the police.

I had no idea that we *had* so many police! As darkness fell, the wail of two-tone sirens as police officers were drafted in from all over the South East was constant.

Fleet Street brought in its battalions. Reporters and television news camera crews sped down from London.

One character was walking about lop-sided with the weight of what appeared to be a large leather handbag on a shoulder-strap. He had a thing like the old-style telephone handset clamped to his ear as he shouted dictated copy to his London news room.

"Haven't you seen a mobile phone before?" he told this incredulous provincial hack. Mobile? Only if you were a weight-lifter…

Part-way through the evening, Jimmy and I were joined by our own reinforcements, reporters Joanne Glazier and John May.

In the centre of the metalwork shop, deep within the compound, were large oxy-acetylene cylinders. Alan Walters, who ran the workshop, had just said: "If those cylinders blow it will be like a bomb…" when a huge flash lit the sky. It was followed by a vast column of smoke and flame. I learned later that the blast was felt in the village of Hooe – two and a half miles away across the fields.

By now the inmate population was divided into two factions – those hell-bent on more destruction and those who feared for their lives.

Fleets of requisitioned coaches arrived. A hole was cut in the wire and a cordon of police and prison officers escorted those who wanted to get away from the riot to the waiting coaches for transfer to less-affected prisons.

By dawn, the last of the rioters had surrendered. Northeye was a smoking ruin.

"I'm going to take a look," Danny said to me. "Are you coming?"

No other journalist covering that event had that "privilege."

As we crunched over the smoking debris, Danny confided his worst fear.

"I think we are going to find some bodies."

There are inner tensions, feuds, vendettas in any prison. A riot provides the perfect cover for revenge. He was wrong and in that respect we were lucky. But in every other respect Northeye was on its knees. Building after building lay in ruins.

The total bill for the nationwide night of rioting was £4.8m. Of that £4.2m had been done at Northeye.

It was *that* big a riot and that big a story. And it had happened on a Wednesday night at a (thankfully brief) time in the Observer's history when we were a Thursday paper. Every national paper and television channel carried the story the next day. We were snookered.

I got home at 7.30am, tired, filthy dirty and on an adrenaline rush. I had done a day's work, then a night's work and now a new day posed an immense challenge.

I bolted breakfast, had a wash-and-brush-up and went to work. We had a quick news conference. There was no option. It had to be an emergency special edition.

Jimmy Burke disappeared into his darkroom to process roll after roll of 35mm film. Jo, John and I began furiously to bang out stories on the typewriters. Stella Graham, then sub-editor, began to plan her pages. By Saturday, we had an eight-page special edition on the streets.

Thanks to Larry Stones' phone call all those years before, I had the inside story on the great Northeye riot. We told how the Board of Visitors had warned the Home Office of the risk of "riot or even death."

Our uncompromising banner headline was: "We told you."

11 Shipwrecks

LIKE your first real kiss, your first shipwreck is something you never forget. Mine was in '64 – shipwreck, that is. One of the first of many kindnesses bestowed by long-serving Bexhill beach inspector John Cruickshank in his career was a timely phone call to tip me off about an impending disaster.

A freighter was on fire from stem to stern off Eastbourne. It was drifting our way. Jimmy Burke and I set off in the firm's clattering Mini Van (then as now, the firm really knew how to spend money lavishly). The pall of smoke grew larger as the Aghios Georgios II drifted towards Normans Bay.

I was totally untrained in how to approach such a situation. But Jimmy conned us a trip in a fishing boat.

The ship, we later found, was laden with esparto grass. Quite what commercial value this has I was never quite sure. But, tinder-dry, it made for a spectacular blaze.

As the fishing boat bobbed closer we became aware of things zipping through the air. They were dropping in the sea around us with a loud fizzing sound.

The doomed freighter's rivets were going off like tracer bullets as her hull glowed red-hot. Jimmy got masses of outstanding pictures. My role for our initial coverage was a mainly a descriptive one.

The freighter beached. Normans Bay – renamed from the previous unappealing Pevensey Sluice after a stranded whale brought it similar temporary fame in the 19th Century – was swiftly thronged with hordes of spectators. The Fleet Street crowd descended en masse, spent their time in the Star Inn and sent off reports of varying accuracy and imaginative flair.

Today, I would have done a Google online search and found all I needed to know about the Aghios Georgios II in moments.

It took me a fair while in the public library to confirm my suspicions. This tub was old – pre-Great War! She had caught fire within sight of land and had been beached without injury or loss to the crew. She was an insurance write-off. All very convenient.

The wreck was national headline news for a couple of days. Then the story cooled, as did the hulk sitting on Normans Bay's shingle.

Covering a good story when it breaks is never enough. The search was on for a follow-up for the next week's edition.

Jimmy and I decided to hammer back over to Normans Bay to see if we could get aboard. By luck, we arrived at the same time as the appointed salvage contractor. He put a ladder against the Aghios' blackened hull and prepared to go aboard with us following close behind.

"Halt for Her Majesty's Customs and Excise!"

The shout came from an officious figure in motorcycling togs who appeared from the top of the beach.

Quite rightly, the law requires that customs officials should be first aboard a wreck to check if there was anything left of value. There wasn't – as our new friend found to his cost.

We got down the ladder. He swiftly ascended and, without a backward (or forward) glance, swung a leg professionally over the gunwhale. With a cry of alarm he disappeared from view.

There is a moral to this story. Where a ship with wooden decks has suffered a severe fire there tends to be a serious deficiency in the deck department.

We found the Customs officer – ash-grey from head to toe – standing in the bottom of the hold spitting esparto grass embers.

Picture opportunities abounded for Jimmy – twisted metal, blackened fittings. Tiring of photographing this, Jimmy as the vastly more experienced hand sent me off to "find something that will illustrate what life was like aboard."

In the burnt-out bridge I found what must surely have been the only document not consumed by the flames. It was the instructions for the fire-extinguisher system.

In later years we had the joys of venturing out on an extremely lumpy sea with the kind-hearted Cllr Ivor Brampton in his speedboat to photograph the General Jacinto. A far larger vessel, she had been badly holed near the bow in a collision off the French coast. But the hole was on the starboard side and could not photographed from land.

No matter how many shots they get, press photographers always demand one more. A life-boat would have been a better craft than a speedboat on a day like that.

I suggested that caution should be the better part of valour. Bomber Command veteran Jimmy scorned this and we put about for another run past the General Jacinto's gaping wound, fully the size of the proverbial double-decker bus.

Too late, I turned to see a huge wave about to engulf us. We got a soaking for our pains that day.

Sometimes luck is with you. "Have you looked out to sea, John?" a contact asked in a call to my home one Sunday when the English Channel was at its stormiest.

"No ... why?"

One look was enough. We have a view of the Glyne Gap area of coast from our bedroom windows. Through the rain and the murk I could see a vessel being tossed about by the waves.

This was another occasion when I took my place with the Press pack, getting soaked and watching a drama unfold. In this instance it was our resident freelance Alan Jones who was photographing the scene.

The story was a strong one. The Tern, a motorized barge built solely for coastal traffic, had broken its back in the gale. The crew had been taken off by helicopter.

Guided by radio by the coastguard, the skipper skilfully brought the crippled vessel through the only small gap in the rocks and beached it. My colleague Andy Hemsley used all his powers of persuasion to get into a Hastings hotel, where the crew members had taken refuge.

He'd thus got a "beat" on most of the nationals and the television crews covering the wreck. I, too, needed an angle.

I am by nature an early-riser. I set off for work at my customary time the following morning. On a whim I returned to Galley Hill. The wreck operation had been coordinated from there by Bexhill's coastguards. The spot overlooks Glyne Gap,

"Sorry you can't come through," said one of two coppers manning the road-block at the bottom of the hill.

"Go ahead, John," said his companion, who knew me.

Another spot of luck. I met up with a contact whose experiences as second officer on a sister ship to the Tern had been of such use to me the previous day.

The Tern's skipper was still aboard. My contact had just been to commiserate with him.

It was low-tide and the sea had abated. My friend offered an old sea-dog's sound advice. If I walked across the sand and if, using the courtesy demanded on these occasions, I called to the skipper for permission and used my contact's name I *might* be allowed aboard.

It worked like a charm. I got my interview on the bridge. I got some pictures of the skipper on the bow.

But the tide was fast rising and the sea was getting up again. By the time I got back to the office with my story and pictures, the Tern was unapproachable once more.

When word got round, the rest of the pack was after what I had obtained. In our game they called bits of luck like that "exclusives".

It is for this type of situation that I had long since developed the practice of keeping a pair of old wellies in the car boot – and an old anorak, old over-trousers, a torch and a pair of ancient Zeiss binoculars for which I had paid £1 in a photographic club auction.

You never know when such things will come in handy.

12 Whitehall farce

ONE of the great joys of journalism is that the unexpected is never far distant. Even the most mundane assignment can have a dramatic twist. Some end with the participants doubled-up in laughter.

Many members of the public have a somewhat exaggerated idea of how a small provincial newspaper operates and how tight are its economic margins.

Equally, some reporters have no concept of the fact that within the Great British Public are some distinctly oddball characters. A few readers harbour the delusion that the story they are about to offer could be worth a lot of money to them.

The young man kept looking over his shoulder as he entered the Bexhill Observer's Sackville Road office. It was as if he believed he was being tailed by some private eye.

"I've got this story for you..." he announced in a stage-whisper; tapping his nose in a secretive way. We explained that we didn't have a large budget to pay for scoops. We didn't have *any* budget for such eventualities, but we were not going to admit that.

He persisted. He had this story. It was a good one. It was exclusive. We continued to try and explain the economic realities of the Observer. If he had a story that was that good he owed it to himself to try and flog it to Fleet Street.

Eventually, he relented. He would tell us anyway. We waited with bated breath.

"I have devised a scientific formula for calculating the cubic capacity of a carrot!"

He watched, expectantly, for our reaction. There was a stunned silence. Eventually, I gathered my senses and explained, diplomatically, that while we didn't consider this to be a story we thanked him for thinking of us.

It took a while to usher him, still protesting the strength of this scoop, from the door. A few days later he was back. The whole rigmarole was repeated – the back-ward glance, the nose-tapping, the thanks-but-no-thanks. Everything.

Again, it was difficult for him to accept his disappointment and leave.

By the third – or was it the fourth – visit our patience was wearing thin. Vainly, I thanked him once more for having thought of us. I had to remind him fairly bluntly that he had been told before that we did not feel that a formula for calculating the cubic capacity of a carrot had any news value.

I played my trump card. Summoning my full mathematical knowledge (a spectacular O-Level GCE failure which produced a 15% mark) I explained that the simpler method would have been to put the carrot in a measuring jug of water and then remove it and take a second reading.

This, of course, would pre-suppose that someone had a need to know the carrot's capacity. The ruse did not work. Eventually, I had almost physically to remove our odd visitor from the office with the stern warning that we did not expect to have the pleasure of his company again.

The whole episode had been stranger than fiction. But then life on a newspaper often is. But there was to be a dramatic sequel.

With a few days our visitor made what we call a "hard" news story. He telephoned the police and asked them to call at his home. He explained he had just killed his father. And he had, quite horribly, with an axe.

I used this true story repeatedly when explaining to young trainees that, in particular when interviewing people in their homes, they should be on their guard.

They all thought I was leg-pulling – until I showed them our cuttings file.

John Liddle later edited the Bexhill Observer. But in his trainee days with us he faced his first important door-step assignment with some trepidation. It was a big story, but a difficult one. If he won the householder over with his persuasive charm in the first few moments at the door-step he stood a (slim) chance of an interview.

On the way to the house he practised what he was going to say. He rang the doorbell. He was prepared. So was the householder.

"Good morning, madam. I'm from the Bexhill Observer. May I..."

"No thanks," said a determined-looking matriarch.

"We use Bronco here!"

So saying, she slammed the door in his face.

I had a rather different experience. We had carried a story which cried out for a good follow-up. Reluctantly, in view of the violent nature of the story and the individual's past convictions, I went to the house.

"Come in, John."

Offered a cup of tea, I chose to accept it in the spirit of getting my story even though I'm a coffee-drinker and never touch the stuff.

The interview went well. He was affable. He explained his side of the story and I left. About a week after we had run the follow-up, a good police "contact" of mine asked: "How on earth did you get the interview with that man?"

I explained.

"And you went in on your own?"

"Sure, how else? Even in those days we couldn't afford the staffing luxury of sending two reporters to one job.

"Why do you ask?"

"Standing orders – we only go there in twos" said my copper friend. "One to interview him and the other to watch for the knife ..."

Lady reporters face an added difficulty. But surely, a diamond wedding interview is the safest possible assignment. Or is it?

Such interviews follow a fairly consistent pattern. The old couple are delighted by the attention. They tell their story with a lot of often-extraneous detail and insist on offering the reporter a slice of celebration cake, a glass of nauseating British sherry – or both.

This one followed the pattern even down to the "what's your secret of a happy married life?" cliché question and the equally cliched "give and take" reply.

The old boy added: "Never looked at another woman in 60 years!"

He repeated this earnest assertion several times.

When the time came for our young lady to take her leave, the old lady remained in her wheelchair. It was the old gentleman who escorted our reporter to the door.

He goosed her bottom outrageously the whole length of the hallway until she was able to release the catch on the front door and make her escape.

Presumably, never looking at another woman for 60 years had been accomplished by closing his eyes and letting his hands do the roaming!

The whistle-blower plays a key part in any reporter's armoury. Typically, this is someone who works in an organisation and seeing things of public importance being hushed-up feels duty-bound to ensure that the public is forewarned.

The local authority, Rother District Council, was in its early days a seething mass of inner tensions. A report was being circulated setting out further internal upheaval. The jobs of top officers were at stake. The council was remaining tight-lipped about the contents of the report. Copies were marked Confidential and numbered.

We were *dying* to get our hands on one.

Fortunately, a whistle-blower rang me. They dare not let me have the report. But if I cared to call at their home their copy *might* be lying open on the table.

Zoom! I was round there. These were pre-digital camera days and I was soon taking down the contents as fast as my left-handed shorthand would allow me.

It was hot stuff. Heads were going to roll.

Suddenly the door-bell rang. My whistle-blower went white. I was in the lounge, the only place where they could entertain another guest. And there was no way out other than the front door.

In a scene straight out of a Whitehall farce I made a dive for the full-length curtains and – making sure to turn my feet to "ten to two" so they did not protrude beneath – hid behind them.

In those days of regular attendance at council meetings I knew every member by voice and had no need to look up from the press bench. I knew the visitor's voice instantly. Another councillor.

"Ah! I see you've got the staff report. Hot stuff, isn't it?

"There'll be *hell* to pay if the Observer gets hold of this..."

How I kept from laughing behind those curtains I will never know.

13 Work and Play

MY big mouth will be my undoing one of these days. Certainly, it has got me into some scrapes. Gerry Clayton brought his own inimitable style to the Observer office - biker style. Gerry loves motorbikes and came to us as a sub editor after years on motorcycle magazines.

"We need to do something special for the start of the speedway season," said Gerry.

"We should get some unsuspecting idiot who has a road licence and sit him on a speedway bike to try it out. If he lives, he could write about it …"

My voice trailed away as Gerry fixed me with a malevolent grin.

It wasn't as if Bexhill had a speedway team. The nearest were the Eastbourne Eagles. But a lot of Bexhillians were keen followers of the Eagles.

That was enough for Gerry.

Arlington's cinder track now stretched in front of us. We had spent an increasingly uncomfortable lunch-time in a Hailsham pub being given some hasty coaching by the Eagles' captain, Reg Trott.

Reg was a kindly man and extremely helpful. But there was no disguising that if Gerry, a highly experienced biker, was a potential lamb for the slaughter I was definitely on death row.

I had been helped into the leathers, felt the unaccustomed weight of the metal-shod boot on my left foot, crammed on a bone-dome for the first time in years.

Now all Reg Trott's advice and guidance was tumbling about my brain. My stomach was a knot of nerves. Two things were a certainty. I was going to hurt myself. And I was going to make a fool of myself.

Speedway bikes have no gears. Worse, they have no brakes. Staying on is a matter of throttle control. Reg had drummed it into us - entering either of the tight oval's two bends you snap the throttle *open*, lay the bike down further than any road-rider would dare and with the rear wheel spraying cinders balance your life on that outstretched metal-shod boot.

This goes against all the rules of self-preservation and requires an effort of will - one which frankly I did not have.

I didn't get hurt. But I certainly made a fool of myself. I was aware of onlookers on that mid-week practice day doubled up with laughter.

In my feature story I likened my speedway style to that of the district nurse on her moped.

I never did conquer the art of letting the back end step out and take a corner in authentic speedway fashion.

Somewhat to my relief, neither did Gerry. To a highly-experienced road biker the whole thing was anathema.

Reg Trott summed it up succinctly afterwards.

"To get the bike set up correctly you have to be doing at least 60 up the straight. If you are doing 60 up the straight and don't set it up right at the corner you go straight into the barrier."

From the start, I had adopted an approach to such journalistic incursions into the unknown. I always told my wife about them.

But *after* the event not before.

Following this dictum, I phoned her from Brands Hatch's Pentagon only after I had enjoyed a day with the Brands Hatch Racing School. This was courtesy of local Ford dealers Hollingsworths, with whom I had done a fair proportion of the many road-tests for our motoring pages over the years.

This treat was lined up by Hollingsworth's John Bargh, a good contact and someone well versed in amateur motor sport.

The principle then was that, after classroom instruction, the novice was taken out by a racing school instructor and shown what an Escort XR3i would do in the hands of an expert.

That stomach-turning experience over, the innocent is then in the driving seat with the expert lecturing on braking-points, clipping-points and racing lines.

You are warned that it is strictly *not* a racing experience but a learning experience.

"Faster, faster, faster! You're not on the school run!"

We were coming up Hailwood Rise faster than I dared imagine. Dreaded Druids loomed ahead of us. Druids, Brands Hatch's hairpin bend, has caught out countless top drivers. Heaven help someone whose yearly motoring mileage was dominated by in-town traffic in a Mark III Cortina Estate.

"You *do* heel-and-toe, don't you?" the instructor yelled as I struggled to comply with orders to brake and come down the gearbox simultaneously.

Heel-and-toe is something I've never mastered. I think my right foot is bolted on my leg at the wrong angle.

Somehow Druids did not claim this Escort as one of its victims. And despite repeated barked orders that a trailing throttle was only for shopping runs and there were only two alternatives on the race track - pedal to the metal or brake hard - I graduated and got a go in a single-seater.

Jimmy Burke's pictures of my six foot frame crammed into a Formula Ford and with an ill-fitting skid-lid on my head tell all.

It was a fun, unforgettable, day and made fun motoring page copy.

But, clearly, James Hunt had nothing to fear.

There were many other race track-days. The South Coast Ford Dealers would hire the lovely Goodwood circuit for a day each year so motoring writers in their post-Goodwood euphoria could extol the virtues of the latest Ford models.

The days would start with coffee and a briefing by Ford executives in the luxurious setting Goodwood House, progress to a morning's track testing and be rounded off by a good lunch back at the house.

Goodwood is typical of many post-war circuits, a former airfield. Unlike hilly Brands, it is airfield flat. This brings its own challenges. It makes judging corners more difficult. I found St Mary's particularly difficult.

"I'll take you out," said Paul Hollingsworth, another noted amateur competitor in his day.

It was an eye-opener. The Grenada was built for company executives. I never dreamt that one could get round St Mary's with such agility.

The after-lunch entertainer one year was a gentleman who walked barefoot on broken glass. The climax to his act was to *jmp* onto bottles smashed by diners to demonstrate that it was not a put-up job.

I felt that I had been on broken glass all morning.

Lancia staged a press day at the Donington circuit to demonstrate their new supercharged models to the Press. Again, a race instructor took you out for a few laps and explained braking-points etc in the manner of a schoolmaster with a cerebrally-challenged child.

Then you were let loose on your own with the stern warning to give way if you saw lights in your mirrors. Only the star guests were allowed to use lights.

The Craner Curves, fast but tricky, were my nemesis that day. Towards lunch, I imagined I had improved somewhat.

Then I saw the lights. Motorcycle champ Barry Sheene, no mean driver either, came past me as if I were in our old Cortina Estate again.

This chapter was prompted by my wife putting one of our favourite classical music CDs on the hi-fi.

"Festival music …" she said with a nostalgic smile.

Despite all the unsocial hours, the disrupted home-life, working on a small provincial weekly has many compensations.

We started in a pre-retirement reverie to muse over the countless happy hours we had spent together, she accompanying me to the more agreeable assignments.

The Bexhill Festival of Music, is a tradition which saw a happy 21st century revival thanks to enterprising ex-professional singer and chamber of commerce president Tony Mansi.

The original De La Warr Pavilion festivals were the work of Bexhill Borough entertainments director Rupert Lockwood and continued after his retirement by his successor, David Blake.

We met Sir John Barbirolli in the days when the famous conductor brought the Halle Orchestra to the festival. We enjoyed the City of Birmingham Symphony Orchestra.

At the after-concert festival club functions we discovered that classical musicians are quite capable of pinching the dance band's instruments during their comfort break and demonstrating their jazz credentials.

The autumn Festival of Light Music traditionally brought the BBC Concert Orchestra to the pavilion. Friday Night Is Music Night went out live to radio listeners.

Councillor Ivor Brampton would organise a charity concert for a deserving cause at the drop of a proverbial hat. Backed by his wife, Maureen, he had the knack of charming both musicians and sponsors into creating occasions that were both memorable and productive.

The local Press is, of course, invited to such occasions for a purpose - to publicise the event. But writing a review is no burden whatever in comparison with the pleasure gained.

There are, inevitably, the odd exceptions.

The first duty of the critic is honesty. There is no future in glossing over something which is not up to the mark. The reader sees through the ploy immediately. The critic can lose credibility instantly.

On their night, Bexhill Amateur Theatrical Society (the BATS) can punch well above their weight. But every company has the occasional flop.

The trick when reviewing is to temper honesty with constructive criticism but I struggled after one particular BATS offering. A poor choice of play had been reflected by a lack-lustre performance.

"There are many domes on the pavilion ceiling," my review began. "I know, I counted every one…"

I cut my teeth as a critic reviewing repertory theatre. For years our resident rep company was the Penguin Players, led by the redoubtable Dicky Burnett and his wife, Peggy Paige.

Rep is demanding of performers. They spend their working lives playing this week's role while learning next week's lines.

It was equally demanding for me. But I found a formula. Slip into the Thursday opening matinee, bag my favourite seat where a chink in the poorly-closed curtains provided just enough light and settle down with a wad of copy-paper bulldog-clipped to the cardboard back of a notebook.

I prided myself that by final curtain I would have the review not only written but subbed and a headline written.

Then it was out into the car park, drive to the Cambridge Road works at Hastings and hand my work directly to one of the Linotype operators.

In those days pavilion catering manager John Gledhill needed to bring in many part-time waitresses when he hosted a major dinner. I think he recruited some of them from the Senior Citizens' Club! The resultant pantomime preceded by many years Julie Walters' wonderful television character. A geriatric waitress would totter over bearing brimming plates of soup in palsied hands. The result was inevitable.

John's nod as I mopped the shoulder of my dinner jacket meant "Send me the dry-cleaning bill - again."

The Pavilion, the Granville Hotel, the Cooden Beach Hotel, Moor Hall Hotel at Ninfield - these were the days when every local society seemed to have an annual dinner. And there were plenty of local societies - sadly many of them gone. The Tradesmen's Ball was a long-held town tradition, as was the mayoral dinner party and the annual dinners of the Chamber of Commerce,

The Scottish Society's Burns Nicht (at which we once saw a president down a full bottle of malt whisky before giving a word-perfect tribute to the Bard and loan me his *first edition* in his trusting state) was complemented by the dinners of the Building Trades Employers' Federation, the Hotels Association and the Independent Schools' Association.

Like the proposers and seconders at the annual mayor-making ceremony at the town hall, which in her time as mayor's secretary my wife would organise, after-dinner speakers vied with each other for verbosity. The trick was to sort whatever "meat" there might be in what they said from the stale jokes and padding that went with it.

Looking back through the Observer's bound files, I find I was sometimes successful in extracting a genuine news angle. Or was it that in those days we had speakers who, despite the length then expected of them, really did have something meaningful and challenging to say?

Ann and I were on a table at right angles to the top table at a chamber of commerce dinner at which the chairman of Rother was guest of honour and principal speaker. Tim Price was a typical farmer. No frills. He came directly to the point. No fancy high-flown phrases. My left-hand flew over the shorthand pages.

After the councillor, a good friend to both of us, sat down, he too began to write. His note, on the back of the menu was duly passed with great solemnity, hand-to-hand along the top table and down our table. Intrigued, I unfolded it.

It read: "Dowling, you look like a bloody Airedale sitting there"

Happy, happy days.

14 Thrusting a blowtorch up the kilt of conceit

THE foregoing personal chapters were written for a number of reasons, not the least of them a little work-therapy at a time of pre-retirement stress and deep unhappiness. The three of us count ourselves fortunate to have spent our working lives in a profession which we love and which in a modest way has served us well.

When I was invited to give a talk on journalism at Pebsham Community Primary School a little lad caused his teachers to go red-faced with embarrassment at question-time.

"How much do you earn?" he asked.

Fair question. I had been blathering on about provincial journalism as a career and, naturally, before troubling his head further the lad wanted to know what would be in it for him if he pursued the black art.

I answered him truthfully. I said I earned just about the national average wage. That is, of course, not a great deal in return for long and deeply unsocial hours.

The lad was clearly unimpressed. As well he might be. The staff were still horribly embarrassed. But I added a further detail.

"I count myself to be a wealthy man."

The lad sat up and took notice. The staff began to breathe again. I counted off my assets on my fingers.

*Loving, devoted parents and, as a result, a happy childhood

*Marriage to a wonderfully loving, and understanding wife, who if she minded the long and unsocial hours never complained about them

*A son who grew up to be more like a best pal

*A daughter-in-law who was brought up in one family of mickey-takers and married happily into another

*Two gorgeous granddaughters

*A job which for more than 47 years I loved and which while not making me materially rich brought job-satisfaction in abundance.

You could see the kids thinking that one through. Either this white-whiskered old git has lost his marbles or he has discovered the mother-lode. Then in a short space of time one element out of that fragile and precious equation vanished.

The 2008 credit crunch, swiftly followed by the 2009 recession, gave the latest of a succession of parsimonious newspaper proprietors the justification for further belt-tightening.

A policy of non-replacement of staff who leave voluntarily is, in essence, a sound one - up to a point. As a means of avoiding compulsory redundancies it has merit. But it can only be pursued for so long before it makes serious and damaging inroads into any organisation's ability to function efficiently.

Then came the compulsory job-losses - transferring part of the workplace to another *county* and requiring those post-holders prepared to make a long and costly daily commute compete for a lesser number of positions.

At one of the lowest points of a miserable end to what had been for all three of us modest but happily-fulfilled careers, Ken McEwan unknowingly summed up in a few words the way all three of us felt.

"You never minded the long hours all the time you could do the job properly. You did so willingly all the time you were keeping your contacts and your readers happy.

"Two of us worked flat-out to do a proper professional job on our sports pages. It is that much harder to do a professional job now."

There was heart-searching, of course, but there was really only ever one course of action for each of us and that was to quit. It was not the way we had wanted to go. But having devoted a working lifetime to doing our bit to build up the circulation and the quality of our papers the thought of being part of their enforced decline was anathema.

One of the disadvantages of having stuck around a job for a long time is that well-meaning folk are apt to fall into the trap of saying foolish things like: "whatever will the paper be like without you?"

This is an unthinking line of thought because the Bexhill Observer had been serving the town for getting on for 113 years by the time I quit. It had been going a long time before Phil, Ken and I joined. I am convinced that, despite changing market forces - not the least the advent over the years of television, free newspapers and latterly instant news availability by website - provincial papers still have a future.

Credit crunch and recession may have been the excuse for savage cuts in reporting, subbing and photography - in other words the essential means of creating a newspaper which faithfully reflects its community - but every recession eventually bottoms out.

When better economic times return, provincial papers will have the up-hill task of rebuilding themselves, of regaining the public's confidence in their ability to give thorough and comprehensive coverage.

To do that they will have to rebuild editorial teams composed of people willing to work long and unsocial hours, not in pursuit of the money about which the little schoolboy was ingenuously inquiring but for the sheer *love* of the job.

We three won't be a part of that process. The torch must be passed to others. But they *are* out there. Through the work-experience process, we have seen many young people with the right qualities - dedication, perseverance, an inquiring mind - who are itching to get into journalism. All it needs is for the places to become open to them once again.

In the meantime, those who are tempted into the vanity of believing as those well-meaning outsiders do that this or that local paper would never be the same after this or that old codger quits would be well to remember the words of an irate phone-caller to the Bexhill Observer.

It happened *many* years ago but in the astringent way of a true friend, my former chief reporter, Deb Scott-Bromley (now the Rev. Scott-Bromley) never fails to remind me of it.

Irate Caller (to Deb but within my hearing): "The ruddy Bexhill Observer has never been the same since that John Dowling left!"

As lessons in life go that has never been equalled.

Epilogue

W HEN my old dad first retired and said he was so busy he wondered how he ever found time for work I thought he was exaggerating.

Now, like countless others before me, I am finding how true his words were. When Phil, Mac and I sat down on a gloriously sunny 2009 spring afternoon not long after quitting journalism, we decided that we should each pen a 500-word addendum to our book giving our first impressions of our life of ease.

So many good-hearted folk were asking if I was enjoying retirement that I felt like stencilling "It's *great!*" on my forehead.

In my farewell piece in the Bexhill Observer I wrote that walking boots, camera, garden and - above all - family awaited my undivided attention.

That first spring was a memorable one in many ways - wonderful weather and catch-up time writ large.

When you work what is euphemistically referred to as "unsocial hours" for 47 years, jobs that other folk do in their free evenings and weekends tend to accumulate.

Prompted by the ever-wise Ann, I set out to "pace" myself in retirement - tempering work in the house and garden with taking country walks, holidays with Ann and lots and lots of time with our beloved granddaughters, Molly and Rosie.

Jimmy Burke had given me some sage advise when Ann gave birth to our son, Paul.

"Sod the job, spend as much time with your kid as you can. They grow up so fast."

I did my best to heed this wisdom. In part it meant Paul coming with me on some of my weekend jobs when he was young. He became adept at drawing raffle tickets with me at public functions.

But I am probably seeing as much of Molly and Rosie now as I did of our own child when he was young.

My taste-buds are returning. So many beautiful meals lovingly cooked by Ann had to be bolted down in order to go to an evening meeting or rush off to a fire or an accident. Now I can sit quietly and enjoy my food.

I am still writing stories for the Observer - albeit unpaid - when organisations with which I am involved make news.

Dear old dad toiled for 40 years as a gas fitter in Bexhill, "carcassing" (installing the gas piping and equipment) in both the De La Warr Pavilion and Bexhill Hospital in the process.

Despite a life of hard work, his devoted care for my mother who bravely battled against arthritis for practically all her married life, and a severe heart condition from the age of 60, he lived to be 100 - so providing me with the most unusual centenarian interview of my career.

By his remarkable (and happy) longevity, the old chap contrived to get his pennyworth out of the SEGAS pension fund for more than 39 years, nearly equalling his work-span in the industry.

If I have an ambition in addition to the customary "health, family and happiness," it is to take my former employers' pension fund for an equally long ride.

I reckon that any organisation which sends a retiree his P45 in the post without a word of thanks deserves it.

Three Men and a Quote
Part 3

The Philip Elms Story

PHILIP ELMS was born at Fern Bank maternity home in Old London Road, Hastings Old Town, on August 15th, 1948. He was the second of three sons born to James and Betty Elms. While London was serving as a stop-gap Olympic city, Hastings was still picking up the pieces after the Second World War. Homes and jobs were at a premium; rationing remained in place. The Hastings and St Leonards Observer, destined to play a major role in Philip's life, had its pagination pegged by newsprint restrictions. Philip's career in newspapers began before his 16th birthday. At 22 he married accountant Barbara Chapman whom he had met through a mutual interest in amateur theatre at Bexhill-on-Sea. They have five adult children, Juliet, Sarah, Matthew, Mark and Victoria. Opportunities to work in the national media arose over the years but Philip preferred the community lifestyle of East Sussex. He worked successively as reporter, sub-editor, sports editor, deputy editor and group production editor and filled in as acting group editor in stints totalling two years. He also made a mean cup of office coffee. After nearly 45 years in the industry he declined a revised role in a company being substantially restructured due to the deep recession of 2009. He lives at Bexhill-on-Sea.

1 Royal Salute

THE day I started work was memorable for the whole country. The BBC Home Service played the National Anthem before the 8 o'clock morning news. It was the Queen Mother's birthday. Sixty-four, bless her.

Tuesday, August 4th, 1964, was a picture book summer's day as I climbed into my new grey suit and headed off to Warrior Square railway station at St Leonards. Briefcase in hand, I took the six-mile journey to Bexhill Central before walking the few hundred yards to Western Road.

School was but a memory.

My baptism in the adult world took me up a flight of stairs to the first floor of the F.J Parsons printing works. Here was the editorial office of the Bexhill Observer. A newspaper of some stature.

In those days two people in five bought a copy ... one of the highest pro-rata rates in the country.

I was eleven days short of my 16th birthday when I made my first appearance in that poky office. A generation later Health and Safety might have had something to say about the conditions. No matter.

The editor was L. J. (Len) Bartley. Old School. Authoritive yet not without a sense of humour. At my tender age I still recognised elements of the headmaster in him. He summoned the latest prefect into his office.

He had interviewed half a dozen grammar school boys for the job of junior reporter (presumably they, too, had spotted the job ad in the Hastings Observer) but chosen me, a mere secondary modern school boy.

I never quite understood why, although LJB chuckled heartily when he discovered my 'uncle' was editor of sister paper, the Sussex Express and County Herald.

Truth to tell, Les Lacey was my great uncle by marriage and I had never met him. Yet I still felt it reasonable to pull his name out of the hat when asked if I had any relatives in journalism. It was a fact and didn't newspapers deal in facts?

I recalled being patted on the head as a nine-year-old and asked: "What do you want to do when you grow up?" I was never in doubt. I wanted to be an actor or a journalist.

The actor bit was no doubt encouraged by my life-saving appearance as Fifo in a Hollington Junior School production of Santa Claus Comes Down the Chimney.

My presence of mind had prevented Santa from falling off the 4ft-high stage as he charged around with his head in his sack. Departing from the script, I grabbed his rear end and swung him back up stage.

As for journalism, where did that come from? A search of two centuries of family archive offers little clue. The great uncle aside, the only relative remotely connected with newspapers was an early 20th century paperboy.

My grandfather, James, was a tram driver who progressed to trolley buses – his usual vehicle becoming tourist bus Happy Harold - while before him were a furniture porter, fishermen and enough labourers to have built most of Hastings' roads and bridges.

My father, Jim, had served as a flight mechanic in the Royal Air Force during the Second World War, becoming a dry cleaner and later a wine department manager in civvy street. My mother, Betty, worked for the aircraft equipment company Short Brothers at Rochester during the war (they married at Chatham in 1944).

Brother Terry, two years my senior, sailed the world's oceans courtesy of the Merchant Navy, only much later to earn his crust playing music on local commercial radio. My other brother Tim, six years my junior, was still at school when I joined the paper, doubtless with little anticipation of the successful Whitehall career awaiting him in the Civil Service.

Growing up, I was slow to develop practical skills and that may explain the leaning towards creativity.

The journalistic notion probably took root while jumping on my bike and doing an evening paper round as a 13-year-old.

Money was tight at home and there was never a possibility of pocket money from my father; he simply didn't have it to spare. Without a bank account (only posh people had those), he paid all household bills in cash.

Every payday he would allocate money to a series of small cardboard boxes kept in the sideboard drawer. The boxes would be labelled rent, electricity, gas, food, insurance and (later in life) car. Meticulous about paying his way, he never owed anyone a penny.

When the baker or rent collector called, my mother knew where to find the cash. It was a simple existence borne out of necessity and a salutary lesson in financial common sense. True, I did not take up the idea of labelled cash boxes but then neither have I owned a credit card.

So for me an evening paper round (I was legally too young to do a morning round) funded the odd cinema trip or bar of chocolate. It also bought me a ticket to see the Tornados perform their current No 1, Telstar, live on stage at The ABC, Hastings, in 1962. Girls in the audience were waiting to see Billy Fury.

Rolling 24-hour news and the internet were prospects unfathomed. But I cannot deny getting a buzz from coming home from school, listening to the latest news bulletins on the wireless, then - if I met my customers at the garden gate - updating the stories in the Evening News, Evening Standard or the Sussex-based Evening Argus.

The Profumo Scandal was a big issue and the August 1963 headlines referred to Dr Stephen Ward's fight for life. This followed a drugs overdose by the society osteopath and one of the key players in a real-life drama that made fantasy pin-ups of Christine Keeler and Mandy Rice-Davies. I was able to tell customers that his death had been announced an hour earlier. Stephen Ward became my first scoop.

The scandal would bring down Prime Minister Harold Macmillan and by the time I was being paid to gather news his Conservative government had just weeks to run before Harold

Wilson ushered in a new Labour era. The urge to convey news was fast developing.

That first floor office in Western Road gazed down on a general print floor. Importantly, the general print floor contained the toilet. My shyness over enquiring its whereabouts meant I made several trips to the local public loo down the road before I discovered relief closer to hand.

LJB welcomed me to the paper. He showed me where I would sit and introduced me to my new colleagues. Mr (Bob) Quayle was the sub-editor. A quiet, slightly dishevelled gentleman, probably in his late 50s or early 60s. Rumour suggested he owned half the Isle of Man (so why was he bothering to work at the Bexhill Observer, my junior reporter mind wondered?).

Shake hands now with Ken McEwan (Mac to his friends). He doubled as chief reporter and sports editor. Wow, that sounds important. And he couldn't be much more than twenty. Here's senior reporter John Dowling. Part of the furniture. Another veteran of a similar age.

Now meet the two ladies, Beryl Parker and Rosemary Arscott. Friendly, but do I detect a competitive edge? And here's John Liddle, shipped in a year ahead of me.

Hark, I hear a Glaswegian voice, swearing and cursing on the staircase. It's Jimmy Burke, a real character and, it transpires, a fantastic photographer. Little did I realise at 15 years and 354 days that I would never work with a better cameraman.

Jimmy would study a scene and immediately visualise how it would translate on to the printed page. For snatch pictures of live incidents he would use people and topography to full advantage. No wasted space in any frame. Even group photographs, the staple of local newspapers, were bursting with vitality.

Add to the roll call the editor's secretary, and you had an editorial team in double figures for a single edition, small town paper (luxury unbounded, as we shall discover). I felt both lucky and privileged to have one foot on the journalistic career ladder. And I was eager to get down to work to justify the company's £6-5s. a week investment.

The nation may have been largely locked into a Swinging Sixties mindset - the Beatles were No 1 with A Hard Day's Night – but the Bexhill Observer had not been persuaded. It dutifully served Western Europe's third oldest population with a traditionalist agenda that was both worthy and comforting. It sold like hot cakes so why change?

One of the first duties of the latest recruit to the paper was to check out the dead. Obituaries are a vital ingredient for any local newspaper and are considered an excellent training area.

As LJB explained, obituary notices are cut out and kept by families for generations. You have one chance to get them right. Succeed and the family will be forever grateful. Mis-spell a name or give a wrong date and there's no going back. You have let down that family.

My role was to visit two local undertakers twice a week to be given the names of the newly dead and their next of kin.

Back at the office I would read the names to the editor. If they were significant players in the business or social community I would make arrangements to visit the family for full details. If they were not – and subsequently were unknown to LJB – I would send out a prepared form to the family, stating that "The editor would be glad to be furnished with details of the late ..."

It was during one of these visits that I saw a corpse for the first time. A funeral director had left open the door between his office and the chapel of rest. Suddenly I was aware of a pale face seemingly peering at me from an open coffin.

Returning from a visit to a bereaved family of a well-known businessman, I witnessed the sharper side of LJB's character for the first time. Because relatives were searching drawers and files for information, I was away from the office for a good two hours. The editor must have thought I'd stopped off for a leisurely cup of tea as he greeted me with a terse "Where have you been?"

"I've been out on the Davis obit," I replied politely if matter of factly.

"Oh," he said, and went back into his office. Later he said to colleague John Dowling: "Did you see the way Philip turned on me? He's got spirit. He'll make it."

LJB was less generous in one of his frequent bust-ups with Bob Quayle and I was privileged to overhear a classic euphemism. The pair had had words in the editor's office. Suddenly Quayle emerged hurriedly and slammed the door. Bartley charged out and roared: "Don't slam the door and be rude to me, Quayle, or you'll be relieved of copy."

Sadly, I was not present when big Mike Storr, a future sub-editor, threatened to wrap a typewriter around the editor's head.

Following the standard style for obituaries was an essential part of my learning curve. There was no work experience in those days; no bombarding a would-be editor with clever prose.

The only experience I could bring to the table was the writing of English essays from my school days which had finished three months earlier.

The step from creative writing to factual news reporting had to be negotiated quickly but with care. A helpful word in my ear from Ken McEwan suggested if I followed Daily Telegraph style I wouldn't go far wrong.

My career was under way and I could not have been more pleased. Secondary school had been a pretty dire experience.

My impression was of a ragbag of mainly inadequate teachers - no doubt grateful for any work they could get in post-war Britain - largely failing to inspire a disparate collection of 400 boys. The learning process seldom reached an intellectual level higher than a series of incomprehensible facts chalked on a blackboard. Discipline was instilled at the end of a 2ft cane.

It was grim preparation for the outside world. The notion that I should become a journalist was greeted with derision. I can still see the sarcasm etched into the faces of two senior staff who should have known better. I knew my ambition was achievable. Equally, I knew my fate lay in my own hands.

There is no doubt that LJB took a chance on me. The job was mine some weeks before exam results came through. My results were hardly worth the wait, although I did, apparently, distinguish myself by securing the rare and (in my household) too often derided Certificate for Proficiency in Arithmetic. I say 'apparently' because, upon enquiry, the headmaster said he 'thought' I had passed it. I await confirmation to this day.

So having sailed into a prized newspaper job at the first attempt, I enrolled at Hastings College for courses in Pitman shorthand and typewriting skills (at my own expense).

The arrival of my 16th birthday meant I could now get around on my pride and joy, a pale blue Vespa 125 scooter, second hand, of course.

It was such a liberating moment in my life. Another two years down the line and I would invest in my first used car, a Ford Anglia, but for now I would settle for wind in my face and power at my fingertips. I felt I was joining a fashionable club at the paper since Ken McEwan and the two Johns were already scooter riders.

Not that scooter riders were universally accepted in society. A colleague called David covered his Hastings patch not only by scooter but routinely attired in full Parka regalia.

He looked suspiciously like the hundreds of Mods who roamed the streets looking to pick a fight with the Rockers in the mid-60s. When a group of 20 of them were rounded up by police and herded into the dock before local magistrates the court clerk dutifully read out names and addresses of the defendants, soon to realise he had one man too many.

"And who are you?" asked the clerk. "I'm the reporter from the Hastings Observer," said David, whose earlier protestations had been ignored.

My name was added to the list for the second ever block release course for trainee journalists at Harlow College in Essex. I was placed in digs with the elderly parents of the college principal, a charming couple who did everything to make this fresh-faced 17-year-old feel welcome. After my weekends spent at home, my hostess would always mark my return on Sunday nights (on the train) by preparing a huge bowl of homemade soup containing large chunks of lamb with tomato, onion, potato and any other ingredient readily available in her kitchen.

The delightful old chap would bring morning coffee to my room and, knowing the nature of my work, would recite the salient points from the morning news. I have never forgotten one of his classic appraisals of world events, delivered slowly in cultured Yorkshire tones: "It's snowing in Sussex and the Shah of Persia's dead."

It was an interesting six weeks especially as I became friendly with a very nice girl at Harlow College. The daughter of an RAF wing commander, she was doing a college course and working part-time at the local Wimpey Bar where she always gave me extra portions.

Apart from shorthand practice, my course was of little value. Sessions in news composition and media law would have been helpful.

Instead we made in-depth studies of the works of dramatists Arnold Wesker and Harold Pinter and environmentalist Rachel Carson. A lot of it appealed to my developing interest in theatre but that was not what my company was supposed to be paying for.

Fortunately, formal training in journalism shaped up considerably over the years. Specialist tutors turned it into a thriving little industry. Even so, in-house training proved invaluable at Western Road and I was never afraid to put in the time and effort to learn from those around me.

On a more cheery occasion than compiling obituaries, I was assigned a job that triggered a lifelong active interest in amateur theatre.

I was to cover a meeting called to merge two long-established troupes, the Bexhill Players and Little Common Drama Group. My aunt and uncle, June and Vernon Roberts, had been prominent with Bexhill Players before they emigrated to Australia. Having reported on the merger, I returned to the venue in a private capacity, joined the newly created Little

Common and Bexhill Players and managed to get myself cast in a play.

So there I was, a journalist *and* an actor ... well, well!

Apart from a murder – and we had one or two of those during my time on the Bexhill Observer – there's nothing quite like a royal visit for engaging public interest. So when LJB proudly announced that the Queen and Duke of Edinburgh were coming to Bexhill as part of a county tour the paper went into overdrive.

We trailed the visit for weeks ... the timetable of events, the route Her Majesty would take through our little town, who would form the reception party at the De La Warr Pavilion?

On the last aspect LJB's mind was racing. He was himself a pillar of the community and, as he was apt to remind us, had covered many royal events in the Sandringham area. That was the clincher. He was invited to join the reception party (a fact that could hardly be ignored when LJB was to write his landmark book, The Story of Bexhill).

Bexhill was keen to embrace the royal visit. Small committees sprung up to make local bunting arrangements. I was invited to join a Little Common group since the royal couple would pass through the village on the town's western outskirts en route to Eastbourne.

The full might of the Bexhill Observer editorial team swung into action in the lead-up to the visit. Come the day most had an essential role to play ... watching the crowd, following the route of the royal party, describing the Queen's outfit and, of course, chronicling events at the all-important reception party.

I managed to stroll up to the De La Warr Pavilion entrance, virtually unobserved, to get a close look as the royal couple walked in; security was effective, if discreet.

It crossed my mind that here was the Queen visiting little old Bexhill – the first reigning monarch to do so - just a few weeks after presenting the World Cup to Bobby Moore and his England heroes. What nobody could know was that a few weeks later Her Majesty would be leading the nation in mourning following the deaths of 116 children and 28 adults in the Aberfan colliery disaster.

Soon afterwards I was able to dash a couple of miles to witness the motorcade slowing, but not halting, as the royal party took in the delights of the patriotically decorated Little Common.

My royal visit role had been passive. I could see other matters needed to be tied up for that week's edition so I largely busied myself with those.

The coffee mornings and autumn sales were still a staple of our weekly coverage. One or two obituaries needed to be compiled. The odd reader complaint about holes in the road or dustbin collections still had to be investigated. Real life hadn't stopped even for the Queen.

My only royal 'appointment' was to help the editor choose the photographs for publication from the superb black and white selection offered by Jimmy. LJB was looking for encouragement. From the impressive display covering his large oak desk, he pointed to a picture showing himself bowing and shaking hands with Her Majesty.

"Do you think I should include this one?" he enquired, fearing any suggestion of immodesty. He dug his right forefinger into his cheek, uncertainty revealed in his expression. His essential question remained unvoiced: *Will young Elms deliver the right answer?*

"Yes, Sir," I replied solemnly (and knowing which side my bread was buttered). "I think our readers would want to see this picture."

It was the first known instance of an editor taking my advice.

On the Saturday morning the Bexhill Observer with its vast royal coverage hit the streets. All the signs pointed to a bumper sale. At about 11 o'clock, LJB summoned me into his office and told me to shut the door.

Oh dear, am I in trouble? "I just wanted to say thank you," he said.

All right, I wasn't in trouble but I was puzzled.

"You don't know why I'm saying this, do you?" he said. "No, sir."

He said: "While we were all absorbed in the royal visit, you quietly ensured that the rest of the paper was in good order. Your contribution has been as valuable as anyone's. Well done."

It was a touching moment back in 1966. Importantly, it was recognition of vital teamwork, a discipline that I endeavoured to hand down to generations of young reporters.

2 Designer Mode

LEN Bartley had a profound influence on my career. Of the eleven editors I served under during nearly 45 years he remains head and shoulders above the rest. He was a newspaper man of knowledge and guile, experience and generosity of spirit. At least that is how he seemed to me; some of the women in the office felt he could be unpleasant and overbearing.

He had quirks, of course. For example, he would never vote in a local election. This was on the basis that if people – his readers – saw him walking into a polling booth they would know he was expressing a political opinion. That, in his view, detracted from his impartiality as an editor.

The fact that his pages were filled with pictures and stories about local Conservatives and that Labour would be lucky to get a look-in even at election time was of no consequence.

Nor was he beyond the odd trick to land a story. He deliberately chose me as the office junior to interview the manager of the local gasworks, ostensibly about his pending retirement.

Once I had gained his confidence I was to throw in a question about the validity of rumours that the gasworks were to close. This was a huge issue at the time, fuelled by speculation that the site was required for a shopping complex.

Seizing the chance to do some real-life acting, I set off, notebook in hand. The result was a front page lead story, revealing that the gasworks, were, indeed, to shut down. The editor got his story. The gasworks manager was embarrassed he may have spoken out of turn. He died soon afterwards.

My journalistic interests were gathering momentum. I was fascinated by the weight afforded to stories, what warranted the biggest headlines, the positioning of stories on the printed page. Soon I wanted to design whole pages.

The reality was that our news pages were largely undesigned in the 1960s. The editor would state his preferences but it was up to the compositors to shuffle the hot metal slugs of type into place. Anything that did not fit was omitted from the paper.

Sport was the exception to the rule, being a chiefly one-man operation and consequently easier to manage. My colleague Ken McEwan had instigated page design in our neck of the woods and when the opportunity came for me to occupy the sports desk I grabbed it.

At 18 I became the paper's first full-time sports editor, succeeding John Liddle who had combined the role with news subbing (Ken by this time had moved on). This meant I not only reported the sports scene but could design my own broadsheet pages.

I adopted a style of clean simplicity; something that would guide the reader effortlessly around the page from the eye-grabbing headline to the single paragraph filler. It wasn't rocket science but I felt I was on the next wave of a pioneering development.

My work was spotted by the editor of our stablemate, the Hastings Observer. John Cornelius approached me amid those slugs of hot metal one press day and asked if I'd be interested in transferring to his title.

"I want you to do for my front page what you do for your back page," he said.

Certainly the Hastings Observer seemed a typographical mishmash of a paper to me, so any changes I made had to represent improvement.

Cornelius had been a highly authoritative senior reporter, promoted to the hot seat upon the early retirement of the renowned but utterly mad Freddie Goodsell.

Like Goodsell, he knew Hastings inside out and had the resources to staff a busy newsroom. But the presentational style of the paper had scarcely developed in the post-war era. That's why Cornelius wanted me. And that's why, with the lure of a few extra pounds in my wage packet, he got me.

LJB did not care for the way the approach to me was made. But he remained gracious and admitted he should have pushed me into new areas to further my career. We parted on good terms. I was still only 20 when I made the switch, yet suddenly I was telling older journalists what I required. If they could not deliver, I'd do it myself.

There was no holding me one week: I wrote the two main stories for the front, took the featured picture and designed the page.

Yes, there was an element of ego about it but, essentially, I was being paid to indulge a hobby. Even when I took a week's holiday I'd often pop into the office on the Wednesday night to do a spot of sub-editing. I craved that midweek fix.

This joint reporter / page designer role suited me nicely for four years. I studied every newspaper I could get my hands on, keen to discover what to emulate and what to avoid. By the time I was approached to take on the sports editorship of the Lewes-based Sussex Express and County Herald I had the confidence to say yes.

The year was 1972 when the international news agenda made heavy reading. The Duke of Windsor, the former king, died and phrases like Bloody Sunday and Watergate entered our vocabulary. Sport made the front pages when terrorists struck at the Olympic Games in Munich. Musically, the Beatles had given up and Slade and Rod Stewart ruled the airwaves.

Here in peaceful East Sussex I had acquired a wife and a mortgage so any move had to be right for me.

The interview, ostensibly conducted by managing director Tim Parsons, was unusual in that I was the one probing into the realities of the job while he was virtually imploring me to take it. It soon became clear I was being offered a pound a week pay rise plus my first company car. We shook hands and the deal was done.

"Thank you very much," he said.

So, eight years after dropping his name at my Western Road interview, I was working under the editorship of great uncle Les Lacey. He was a kindly, jovial chap, very much the community journalist.

Unlike some editors of my acquaintance, he had a working knowledge of the local sports scene and was just as concerned that we should cover a Brighton League Division 7 football team as, say, Lewes FC, occupying the lofty heights of the Athenian League. We worked well together until a heart attack forced him to stand down. Never once was our relationship mentioned.

Seven years of criss-crossing rural Sussex covering non-league football, cricket and darts - and most importantly producing weekly pages - had its appeal and I always tried to accept invitations to do guest-speaking at dinners, usually on the theme of what my job entailed.

It's amazing how writing speeches for such occasions can snap you out of any complacency.

Yet it was hard to escape the view that here was a paper, created for the agricultural market of the late 19th century, that had lost its identity during sprawling urban encroachment. It now endeavoured to serve several small towns from Lewes to Rye and Newhaven to Uckfield with countless villages en route.

These places deserved a decent news service but, increasingly, the Sussex Express was not equipped to provide it. With the decline of agriculture there was no replacement peg to hang it on.

A new era under fresh tabloid editorship was underway back on my old stomping ground at the Hastings Observer. In 1979 Peter Welham needed a trustworthy replacement for his excellent sports editor Ken McEwan, now moving on to pastures new at Eastbourne. Welham dangled my first three-figure weekly wage and a company car. I was persuaded.

Sport remained essentially a one-man operation at that time but at least the responsibility was coupled with flexibility. If sometimes I only managed one day off in a fortnight I could still arrange my work schedule around family life (I was now a father), and running an amateur theatre company.

A heady diet of Southern League football, National KO cricket plus international festivals in angling, snooker, darts and table tennis kept the paper's sports content vibrant and meaningful. When Hastings Sports Council was set up as a pressure group there was usually a good row going on somewhere and far be it from me to douse the flames.

The football coverage of Hastings United and subsequently Hastings Town was often fun in the '80s. The one drawback in those pre-website days was that after a Saturday afternoon in the Press box you had to wait until the following Friday before your words of wisdom could be published.

Match reports, therefore, needed to be factual for the record but sufficiently entertaining to be readable so long after the event.

I concentrated our football coverage more and more on what was going on off-the-field: club issues, the on-going battle for financial survival, the managerial merry-go-round, the comings and goings of players. These were, after all, the talking points among supporters at the pub.

Some club managers, such as Gerry Boon, Peter Sillett and Jack Dalton, readily embraced the role of the local Press and were always good copy. They spoke willingly, confidently and often with a twinkle in the eye. A few revealed themselves as surprisingly sensitive souls and preferred to keep the Press at arm's length.

Boon provided one of my favourite managerial quotes. A new young winger had endeared himself to supporters with his electrifying pace. After his debut I commented, "He's quick, isn't he?" Gerry paused for a moment, then said, "Yes, he is quick. All I've got to do now is teach him how to take the ball with him."

It wasn't all fun. Often I would be criticised for treading on club sensitivities and revealing rather more than they would wish to see in print. But I felt that was a strength of our coverage.

Our independence of the club was evident, a point emphasised when I was banned from the Hastings ground in a dispute over access to players for comment. In return we stopped all club coverage beyond a basic results and fixtures service. The arrangement lasted several weeks. Not a single reader complained. Eventually the club chairman, Joe Riordan, resigned and I was invited to resume normal coverage.

It was a sad chain of events but indicative of the friction which can occur when two parties stubbornly defend their respective corners.

In another effort to get over my instant reporting dilemma I adapted my amateur theatre skills to do live match reports on local radio. It involved calling the Brighton studio with team news, goal flashes and half-time and full-time reports. It was unpaid work but another string to my bow.

Mostly these live broadcasts passed off without incident. One exception was a snowy afternoon at Dover. The available phone was attached to an outside pole, yards from the pitch. As the moment arrived to begin my update, I realised my jaw was frozen stiff. What emerged from my mouth sounded more gibberish than usual. I frantically rubbed my face to try to restore some feeling while at the same time offering a breathless account of how the game was going.

As senior football evolved in the town, I witnessed the extraordinary rise and fall of Stamco FC.

From small beginnings on a village green, the club became the talk of the county as seemingly unlimited funds brought a string of still-fit ex-League players to the local scene to sweep aside all opponents on the field: among them Brian McDermott (Arsenal), Jimmy Gilligan (Swansea City), Mike Trusson (Bournemouth).

One summer Steve Gatting dropped nine leagues to join Stamco from Charlton Athletic. It was fantasy football turned reality and all underpinned by millionaire timber merchant Leon Shepperdson. Like all fantasies, it was unsustainable and the bubble burst eventually.

Local newspapers always perform a delicate balancing act between providing a quality service to readers and reporting good results to share holders. When times are hard newspapers get the message early; advertising dries up and owners start off-loading staff.

That is why I accepted deputy editor status in the mid-80s with the proviso that I stayed with sport.

My thinking was that if push came to shove a deputy without a clearly defined day job would be the first out of the door, whereas every paper needed a sports editor.

Russell Claughton, a one-time Fleet Street feature writer and now occupying our editor's chair, accepted the rationale.

A good working relationship ensued. He had a trusty lieutenant and I had a foot in the management door.

A bonus of my dual role was that I suggested I should compile an A4 picture special of a devastating hurricane under the title The Great Storm of '87.

Putting in extra hours while still producing sports pages, I brought together 120 black and white photographs that had already been published in the Hastings and Bexhill Observers. Janette Gould and John Dowling contributed the stories of how the two towns coped. The pleasing result was a 30,000 sale at 65p a time.

A sporting special appeared the following year. To mark the 40th anniversary of the then defunct Hastings United (which coincided with my own 40th birthday) I produced a glossy A4 publication called Claret and Blue.

It contained nostalgic stories and reprinted match reports – principally by Ken Simpson, Ken McEwan and myself – from the club's controversial formation in 1948 to the FA Cup glory days of the '50s and the inevitable cash crises of the '60s and beyond which sparked its demise in 1985.

Unlike the storm publication, an in-house effort, Claret and Blue went out to a local print firm whose technology was considered state-of-the-art, certainly streets ahead of ours. Local newsagents sold most of the 1,500 copies as stocking fillers that Christmas. The perfect gift at £1.95 a time!

I retained the dual role through changes of editor until I finally relinquished sport in 1995 in exchange for the newly created title of group production editor.

So many dramas lay ahead ... and we are not talking amateur theatre!

3 Legal minefield

REDUCING staff numbers to keep costs in check has been a regular ploy by successive owners down the years. Technology may have simplified some procedures but without sufficient reporters to gather the news, papers can slip into the trap of 'easy copy.' Instead of investigating serious issues that affect people's lives, space is quickly filled with a ready diet of courts, council meetings and chasing ambulances.

From the Hastings days of my youth the reporter headcount has shrunk from about 15 to four or five, always assuming reporters hang around long enough to be counted.

Here's an extract from my 1998 diary during an editor's absence:

February 2: Young Indian reporter Arup joins today to cover Battle area.

February 3: Arup resigns to take up offer from Peterborough Evening Telegraph.

February 4: Arup leaves today with rail fares in lieu of salary.

February 9: Editor Richard Neale, back from holiday, says: "How's Arup getting on?" I say: "You're not going to believe this ..."

From the mid-90s to my last working day I had overall responsibility for ensuring our titles were produced to a good standard and delivered down the line to the printers on time. These were the Hastings, Bexhill and Rye / Battle Observers. Each title had its own sub-editor. I took on the Bexhill title, while retaining the deputy editor role at the Hastings title.

The editor's role had become mainly managerial ("Budgets and fire extinguishers," we used to say), although he could, of course, influence any area. Every editor has little foibles which must be indulged (favourite / least favourite townspeople to be publicised generously / cautiously; favourite / least favourite business / charity, ditto). I much preferred my role.

Although I had stood in for absent group editors for a total of more than two years, the ultimate editorial position never appealed.

Only on one occasion was I tempted to apply for the editorship and that really was to gain first-hand knowledge of current interview procedure. My sole previous interview had been the schoolboy experience back in 1964. Luckily, editors had approached me regarding all future roles.

My 2005 application was far from frivolous but as I confided to a colleague: "I'll be pleased if I get it and relieved if I don't."

The interview was conducted perfectly fairly by two very senior company figures, who were clearly seeking someone to take up the managerial reins, not an editorial production figure. It proceeded along traditional lines with boxes being ticked (or not). More than ever convinced that this job was not for me, I made my move with a rehearsed interjection.

"Look," I said, "we all want the same thing, don't we? We all want to produce cracking good papers that sell like hot cakes. I can do that. I'm your man. Give me the job and you won't regret it."

There was a pause. Two pairs of eyes glazed over. I sensed neither of the interviewers wanted to be the first to respond. Eventually one said softly: "Quite."

It might have been the public perception of what an editor does but we all knew the reality. I couldn't wait to get back to the day job. The budgets and fire extinguishers would be someone else's baby.

The postscript to that episode was that the preferred candidate turned down the position (perhaps he had just discovered the salary), leaving yours truly to hold the fort for more than three months until an appointment was finally made.

It was the most stressful period of my career. I was compelled to keep the production schedule on track, while taking calls from the public, tip-toeing through legal matters and attending management meetings. Effectively, I was doing two full-time jobs simultaneously. Senior colleagues were enormously supportive but I knew the ultimate burden was mine. A new editor came through the door not a moment too soon.

A key aspect of being in charge was not so much attending management meetings but being mindful of legal constraints in our reporting. Fighting against the clock is no defence if you mess up. Two national stories needing close scrutiny broke on our patch in 1998.

There is often little of substance to report in the first few weeks of a New Year. The world – or at least our corner of it – is still emerging from party season lethargy.

That mid-January the Hastings Observer's main page one story was destined to be an account of Lord Attenborough's visit to the town to discuss his up-coming film project about Grey Owl, a local folk hero. There was a suggestion the film's star, Pierce Brosnan, might show up, an opportunity the girls in the office felt we shouldn't miss.

Then at 8.30am on the Thursday - press day - we received word that a man had been shot dead by police at St Leonards. While news editor Ann Terry and senior reporter Sandra Daniels delved into the story, Lord Attenborough was cleared from the front page, together with some expansive artwork promoting a tenpin bowling offer. Our team did an excellent job and we went to press on time with the editor's headline that screamed: *Man, 39, shot dead by cops.*

We added 2,000 copies to the print run in anticipation of a bumper sale prompted both by the shooting and the big sports story of the week, the sacking of Hastings Town football manager Garry Wilson.

Two telephone complaints were received about the use of the word cops in the headline; this was considered an offensive term akin to pigs. Curiously, no-one had complained when bollocks appeared in a story.

The shooting story gathered momentum by the day. My diary recalls: "As we prepare the follow-up story, a man turns up in reception to offer photographs of the dead man. I accept his pictures but he wants one used alongside a positive story on the death of his acquaintance. I consult Richard (the editor). I persuade the man we sincerely want to publish a positive story. That's good enough for him. 'I can tell by your voice you're an honest man,' he says. What would he have said if I didn't have a cold, I wonder?"

But the story was not over yet. We knew early on that the dead man was James Ashley, a name that would haunt Sussex Police for the next decade as the rights and wrongs of the killing repeatedly returned to the courts.

Here is that week's press day diary entry: "Main discussion in the office is whether we should name the 18-year-old girl in bed with the naked man when he was shot. Two staff members are virtually certain they know her identity. No official source will confirm it. If we're wrong we are in deep trouble. We cannot take the risk. Then comes another twist.

"A man arrives in reception, trembling and fearing for his life. He admits he's a former drugs dealer who's served eight months of a 15-month sentence.

"Now he's a barman in a bar frequented by the drug psychos. A copy of the picture we have can be seen in his bar and he says it's already caused problems with the drugs gang. He says he'll be next for a knifing if they think he gave us the picture.

"I give him certain assurances to allay some fears (can't say too much, even in a diary) and he leaves with handshakes all round. In the course of conversation he mentions the girl's first name; it corresponds with the name we have. So we add a paragraph to our lead story, referring to 'Jimmy and Caroline's relationship.'

"Thankfully, pre-press are way behind schedule due to staff shortages and a late stoning for page 1 brings no added problem."

Another huge story that year demanding careful attention concerned the murder of a 13-year-old schoolgirl, Billie-Jo Jenkins. Her foster father, Sion Jenkins, a respected deputy head, was charged. The story attracted blanket coverage both locally and nationally. I neither wrote nor sub-edited the story, but wearing my deputy editor's hat, I agreed to be interviewed by Sky News on the town's reaction to the killing.

An indication of how this story found its way to the breakfast table via the Hastings Observer is contained in a diary entry I wrote on press day:

"While always mindful that we are dealing with a great human tragedy, journalists need to operate dispassionately as they cover unfolding events.

"This can trigger tensions between national and local Press, the nationals playing up Hastings' decadence and ourselves trying to fight off such stereotypical images. Often we fight a losing battle.

"Under the laws of the land nothing that might be prejudicial to the trial can be written or broadcast ahead of the verdict. But the delayed trial of Sion Jenkins gave ample time for nationals and local alike to prepare their background pieces.

"So how were we to cover the trial? Long gone are the days when the Hastings Observer editorial staff numbered 15 or more. We can now conjure up five reporters if you include the news editor and the (mainly) leisure reporter.

"We had the good fortune of a tie-up with one of our former reporters, now advancing his career with an East Sussex-based agency. In return for free access to our files, Gary Lucken was able to work for reduced rates to cover the Jenkins trial at Lewes Crown Court.

"It lasted three weeks and generated copious copy – the prosecution case, the defence, the jury's long deliberations and the verdict.

"The most tense aspect occurred yesterday when the jury began their deliberation. Normally we have until noon on a Thursday to button things up and send the front page down the line to Eastbourne. We anticipated a verdict today but for us to go to press without it would be folly. We negotiated a later print slot. We heard the judge had given the jury until 4.30pm to reach a verdict by a majority decision, otherwise he would order a retrial.

"With time fast passing we prepared a front page for three scenarios: Guilty (Evil bastard gets life); Not Guilty (My agony over by innocent deputy head); and Retrial (Jury couldn't make up their minds). Backgrounders were now in type.

"The call we were waiting for arrived at 3.30pm. The unanimous verdict was Guilty. The right pages were assembled in the right order – a demanding piece of work under such time pressure. Five pages of trial coverage are ready. Guilty, screams the front page headline.

"The verdict hit national radio and TV news bulletins immediately. The Nine O'Clock News and News at Ten both headlined the story.

"The Hastings Observer became a protected paper within our centre. Nothing was allowed to stop it getting on to the streets on time. And nothing did.

"A brilliant piece of work by editorial and production staff. The result was an average 22,500 weekly sale boosted to 24,000-plus."

My diary note concluded: "The horrific nature of the killing took something of a backseat as the editor sent champagne into the newsroom to toast a job well done."

Yet this was the story that would never quite go away. Following appeal, Sion Jenkins became a free man as two retrials proved inconclusive.

For all the drama of maximising the impact – and sale – of that edition, preparation had been essential. It wasn't always so. Here's another diary entry from the late 1990s:

"It's been another long production week but, being Thursday, I'm clearing off to do the school run. But wait. Another crisis looms.

"Sandra realises a court report in the Hastings Observer would be unlawful as an alleged burglar she was told was 19 is in fact 17 and probably should not be named for legal reasons.

"I put a late call through to pre-press at Eastbourne, explain our predicament and persuade an understanding machine boss to cut the page negative, so obliterating the offending reference.

"We're just in time and the company avoids a potentially costly legal bill. I'm 20 minutes late picking up the kids but some choccy bars make up for it."

Many changes in technology have been embraced over the years, some more successfully than others.

The fundamental switch from hot metal to computer-set was overseen in the 1980s by a newly created owner company called Senews (a hybrid of South East News). There was something of the pioneering spirit here, not least by Robert Breare's group of entrepreneurs who had the skill and energy to back their investment.

Life on the paper was seldom less than exhilarating. An ITV crew spent weeks with us making a series called The Press Gang. Staff from all departments were generously featured with special emphasis on the new state-of-the-art press hall at St Leonards.

I was shown interviewing young Hastings footballer Kevin Ball who was moving on to pastures new (some years before he became captain and subsequently acting manager of Sunderland). A lengthy but untransmitted interview with me about my job as sports editor remains a collector's item!

Hi-tech changes under later owners were sometimes introduced too hastily: pages appeared ink-smudged or even blank, duplicated or inadvertently placed in the wrong paper. One reader observed that the mistakes were the talk of the bingo club.

Mistakes are also the talk of the estate agency community if their lucrative advertisements are affected.

Press hall errors were regrettable if understandable as staff got to grips with new work practices. Computerised production in those early days was a disaster waiting to happen.

A sister paper of ours actually hit the streets one winter's morning showing a front page from the previous August. In the usual race against time to produce the paper no-one had spotted the most basic of errors.

Not that we were immune from mistakes, ourselves. I am personally guilty of duplicating stories and pictures, usually the result of cut and paste procedures. And I confess to a few nonsense headlines where a midway change of thought has gone undetected.

Literals (typos) are an unwelcome but inescapable fact of newspaper life. I long ago disciplined myself to double check the spelling of 'count' and 'county.' Alas, I have not always been vigilant when a reporter, through a slip of the keyboard, has omitted the fourth letter in 'public.'

Not that such slips are anything new. One of the tales L. J. Bartley enjoyed re-telling concerned the Victorian reporting of a royal trip up the Thames: "The crowd applauded enthusiastically as the queen pissed under the bridge ..."

Lots of things irritate readers and, obligingly, they will always point out our failings. The type is too small. Pages too heavily inked. Too much football coverage. Not enough football coverage. One of the crossword clues is missing. And, of course, typographical errors: "Don't you employ proof readers?" "Well, no actually."

A regular complaint comes from the criminal fraternity who seem to think we need their permission to publish their names in court cases.

"Er, excuse me, Dr Shipman: we'd be awfully grateful if you'd allow us to publish your name ..."

4 Beginners, please

L OOKING back on some 40 years in amateur theatre, I can see the hold it has had on my life. 'My life' are the key words here because my family, my career in journalism and my theatrical interests are inextricably linked.

The on-stage activities have produced exactly the same stresses and strains as other aspects of life.

Having appeared in more than 50 plays and given some 150 performances - ranging from the Little Common and Bexhill Players in the 1960s through to Rother Theatre Company in the 21st century - I am certainly not proud of every production I have been involved with. Equally, there have been a lot of good times.

I saw my first pantomime at the age of five. I was taken to see my Uncle Vernon and Aunt June in a Bexhill Players production of Babes in the Wood at Bexhill Amateur Athletic Club. Later I dabbled in drama at junior school and performed sketches at youth club.

My only noteworthy achievement at senior school was to get cast as the editor (how appropriate) in a production of George Bernard Shaw's Androcles and the Lion at the age of 15. I wanted the part of Androcles but the teacher's pet got it instead (even if I did have to surreptitiously prompt him while on stage). Still, he went on to become a university drama lecturer so I suppose he must have come good in the end.

My newly started journalistic career with the Bexhill Observer brought me happily into contact with the Little Common and Bexhill (LCB) Players and I soon found myself learning lines. The play was a drawing room comedy called Silver Wedding, by Michael Clayton Hutton.

Two of us were interested in playing the part of the son of a couple undergoing a relationship crisis after 25 years of marriage. In addition to myself, there was a chap named Nigel on the scene whose claim to fame seemed to be that he'd once had a minor role in a TV serial called Coronation Street which had started a few years earlier. The producer, the veteran actress Ada Clutton, chose me.

Silver Wedding was a well-constructed, if formulaic, comedy that entertained our audiences at the De La Warr Pavilion in that early summer of 1966. It was a happy production. Graham Miller and Pat Bruce (both experienced campaigners) welcomed me to the fold and fellow cast members Sally Wells, Pam Blake-Wilson and Clara Webb were a joy.

As my stage experience developed I always prepared well, felt relaxed, in control ... up for it. Confident but never, I hope, complacent. And being mindful that audiences were paying fair money to be entertained, I felt that was a good trait.

Doing the rounds of comedies, dramas and thrillers suited me well enough although I have never been a song and dance man. So when my LCB colleagues spread their wings to include variety shows, they asked me to be compere. I even gave our first De La Warr show its title ... A Little Bit of Common (clever, eh?).

I would fill in for a couple of minutes while the next act was lining up behind the curtain. I cribbed an idea from The Frost Report, a popular TV show of the time, in which David Frost and Ronnie Barker would rattle off amusing news items. I scripted my own local material and varied the content from performance to performance, depending on audience reaction.

Between the matinee and the evening performances on the Saturday I was sitting in my dressing room trying to think of something fresh to say that night.

Suddenly an idea occurred. It had been announced in that morning's Bexhill Observer that the vacated RAF Station (Wartling) at Little Common was to be turned into a prison. This news was both big and controversial.

Knowing that a fair portion of Bexhill Council would be present for our last night, I jotted down on my script pad: "It was announced today that a new training centre for councillors is to be opened at RAF Station (Wartling)."

Now I quite agree that joke has not stood the test of time. But for that precise moment in history it had the desired effect.

The audience rocked with laughter. Fellow cast members waiting in the wings heard the audience erupt. "What did he say? What did he say?" they demanded to know. Eventually I would tell them: "Oh, it was a just little one-liner I slipped in."

Cool or what?

Only once did I stray from the compering role in a variety show. I put together a little Christmas scene in which I narrated the Roy Orbison song, Pretty Paper, with three girls singing the chorus and a young actor portraying the street salesman. Hopefully, the audience found it less excrutiating at the time than it seems to me in retrospect.

My early years with the LCB Players were a time of youthful exhuberance. We would just go along, rehearse our scenes, meet friends, have a laugh ... in fact we only seemed to get serious about the job in hand once the playdates approached. And, to a man and woman, we were deadly serious about giving of our best on stage.

We felt we owed it to the company, to our audiences and, indeed, to ourselves. That certain inner belief had to be present. I always felt if I couldn't give a competent performance, then wild horses wouldn't drag me on to a stage.

That is not to say everything always went to plan. Indeed, the old adage "Anything that can go wrong will go wrong" might have been created for the theatre.

Every amateur production is fraught with risks. Understudies are virtually unheard of; you try getting someone to learn a part knowing he is unlikely to reach the stage. And with plays cast three or four months in advance the threat of illness or family bereavement is one that must be addressed.

I recall one leading lady whose mother died unexpectedly during a three-night run by Bexhill Amateur Theatrical Society (BATS). The company were prepared to cancel. Stoically, our actress insisted on carrying on.

A more avoidable problem was illustrated by a professional actor friend. He told a story from his repertory days when his troupe were performing by night and rehearsing the following week's play by day. One night he and a fellow cast member were locked in dialogue when both became aware they had lurched into the following week's play. They managed to talk themselves back into the right play. There seemed to be no post-performance reaction, which makes me wonder how carefully audiences actually listen to the dialogue.

I was still youthfully irresponsible when, as a member of the BATS, I became a passion killer at the De La Warr Pavilion. As the romantic leads prepared themselves for a warm embrace in the second act, the woman was supposed to lift the lid of the gramophone and play a suitable piece of music.

As a mere juvenile character (in more ways than one) I decided to cool their ardour one night. The woman in question lifted the gramophone lid to see a hand-written note on the turntable. "Your knickers are falling down," it said.

She fought to quell the giggles. The kiss she was about to share was a spluttering disaster. "If I find out who did that, I'll scrag him," said her stage lover. Nobly, I owned up to save fellow cast members from suspicion.

Interestingly, as I grew older and became involved in company administration and stage management, I took firmly against any kind of practical joke on stage and would "scrag" anyone I felt had let the side down, although, in truth, it seldom happened.

Mind you, the point can be reached where you're just happy if the actors turn up. In the old Bexhill rep days, Richard Burnett would be seen on his favourite stool in the Devonshire Arms. At about 8.20pm he'd look at his watch, put down his glass and say: "Well, I must be off; I'm due on stage in 10 minutes." He would then coolly walk down to the seafront, through the theatre's stage door and straight on stage.

Some actors are marginally less dependable. One veteran actor of my acquaintance failed to realise there was a Saturday matinee and had to be extricated from a nearby local coffee shop and shoved on stage with not a moment to spare.

I had switched my allegiance to the BATS in 1968. Their concentration on plays rather than variety shows appealed to me. A young woman in the society also appealed.

Communication with her had begun a year or two earlier. As LCB secretary I had occasional correspondence with Miss Barbara Chapman, the BATS' treasurer. Only when I heard her engagement was off did I dare to make my move.

I told Barbara I was going to review Kings Rhapsody at the White Rock Pavilion for the Hastings Observer and would she like to come with me? She said yes. We hit it off from there. Our engagement was announced at an after-show party on stage at St Peter's Community Centre where we had first met. We were married at St Mary Magdalene's Church on February 20th, 1971. She's been my rock ever since.

As ever, theatrical societies seemed to suffer a shortage of young male actors. My arrival within the society widened the scope of plays that could be presented. I appeared in half a dozen plays on the bounce, portraying virtually the same character in different guises.

After two solid years of walking around with a script in my hand I was ready for a break, fun though it had been.

Numbers attending plays were beginning to wane (and not simply because I was making so many appearances). Action was needed. Although I had dabbled with direction, I seized an opportunity when it arose, persuading the society to let me direct Suspect, by Edward Percy and Reginald Denham.

A key attraction was that the play was loosely based on one of the big news stories of the 1930s, the Lizzie Borden axewoman case.

"Let me direct it," my argument went, "and I'll publicise it for all it's worth in the paper and around the town." I reckoned we could attract a four-figure audience for the first time in donkey's years.

The BATS committee agreed to my slightly cheeky suggestion and suddenly I was making my pavilion debut as director. It was a huge responsibility, of course, but one that I accepted with all diligence. Now I knew how George Bernard Shaw must have felt when he directed his play, The Millionairess, at the same venue four decades earlier.

I was able to cast Suspect strongly and the set designers did a superb job. 'Gripping drama' and 'based on true events' were phrases central to the publicity. Audiences turned out in their biggest numbers for years.

Agonisingly we fell short of the magic 1,000-patron mark by about thirty but the public and society alike were happy with the quality of the production and that was always paramount.

New ideas were buzzing in my head. Having set up home in the Pebsham area of Bexhill, I was soon toying with the notion of establishing a district theatre troupe. Some good people came forward to offer their services and Pebsham Players came into existence in the autumn of 1974.

During this energetic period I became a governor of Pebsham County Primary School (my sports day one-to-one sprints with headteacher Bob Platt were enthusiastically cheered by the pupils, especially when Bob scraped over the line ahead of me).

As vice-chairman of Pebsham Community Association, I played a prominent role in setting up the allied Pebsham Sports and Social Club, of which I was appointed a trustee.

To ensure there was genuine demand for such a club, a few of us rang hundreds of doorbells as we embarked on a mammoth survey of the area. The vast majority of householders offered a positive response. Happily, the club thrives to this day.

There were various scary moments during my early times with Pebsham Players. We rehearsed and played at St Michael's Community Centre, a converted school gym with no visible theatrical attributes.

That meant creating a stage with platform blocks and rigging up a makeshift proscenium arch and lighting. Operating under the terms of a temporary theatres licence meant the stage curtains had to be flame-proofed to the satisfaction of the Fire Service.

This was the drill every time we performed there, sometimes working till two or three in the morning. It was all pretty exhausting. But I could have done without one experience. I was fixing the lights close to the ceiling when my ladder slipped. I made the fastest stage entrance of my life and, all these years later, still have the scars to remind me.

I recall those St Michael's shows with great affection, especially when we had to put up the House Full signs. We were limited to 80 or 100 people per performance, depending on the terms of the theatres licence of the day. Yet we managed to attract appreciative audiences who would come back time and again, hopefully because they knew they would see a decent production at a reasonable price.

Even so, accidents and disasters lay in wait.

5 The show must go on!

PEBSHAM Players had assembled some fine on-stage and off-stage talent. Town mayor Cyril Carpenter was sufficiently impressed to arrange for us to mark our tenth anniversary in 1984 with a production at the De La Warr Pavilion. It was the start of a happy relationship with the pavilion and, indeed with the district council, who had agreed to grant-aid us.

All went more or less smoothly until the roof fell in. We opened one October evening in 1987 with Emlyn Williams' appropriately titled thriller, Night Must Fall, which I was directing. The always-stressful first performance had gone well; actors in spirited form, the stage crew right on the button. What could possibly go wrong?

Well, how about a hurricane striking? It ripped a hole in the pavilion roof. Sea salt and filth whipped up by the wind made a complete mess of the set and the theatre had to be closed for safety reasons. Entertainments supremo David Blake rang me first thing in the morning with the sad news.

"But David," I pleaded, "the show must go on." Of course, in real life, the show can't go in these circumstances.

So we kept the production on ice and started again in our next pavilion slot the following spring. Playgoers were aware of the hard-luck story and gave us a fantastic reception.

Another time misfortune struck was on the occasion of a theatrical experiment in the early 1980s. We embarked upon a joint production with St Peter's Players. The play was the Jean McConnell fishing comedy, Haul for the Shore.

My job was production co-ordination, effectively looking after all aspects of the show, without responsibility for directing the play.

Such a joint venture had all the makings of a theatrical disaster as egos set out on a collision course. We were prepared to tread on eggshells if necessary.

Then ... disaster. The weekend before curtain-up leading man Peter Stacey slipped a disc in his back and had no chance of recovering in time. Guess what? They sent for Muggins.

Fortunately, production arrangements were largely in hand and, on this occasion at least, I didn't have to double up as stage manager. As always, my intention was not to go on stage and perform wonderfully well, it was to avoid making a complete prat of myself. Over that hot weekend I spent 22 hours learning a part which, frankly, I wouldn't have auditioned for. But needs must ...

My first full rehearsal was the dress rehearsal, then it was straight into a three-night run. Additionally, there was a Saturday matinee to be survived.

There we were, acting our hearts out in the middle of a heatwave and dressed in thick woollen jumpers. The sweat fairly dripped. It was the best weight-loss plan I'd ever experienced.

But, supported by a strong team, I got through without mishap. Director Jack Baker voiced his appreciation. "You thrive on pressure," he said.

The sort of stage performance in which I and countless others have been active has its roots in The Kursaal, a major seafront entertainment centre during the late 19th and early 20th centuries. There was something on virtually every day of the year and the venue helped establish Bexhill as a significant tourist resort.

Enterprising young company manager Philip York sparked the town's renowned reputation for repertory by presenting regular plays at the Kursaal.

In later years, during seasonal breaks in the professional repertoire, the amateur troupes would feed an insatiable appetite for plays at venues such as Egerton Park Theatre or the De La Warr Pavilion. Community centres subsequently provided more intimate settings.

The venue dictated the style of acting. A small arena meant eye movement and slight hand gestures were often key to establishing a character. The cavernous pavilion demanded more flamboyant movement and a projected voice, we were told, that could be heard by the deaf old lady in the back row.

Quite why a deaf old lady would park herself in the back row we never quite fathomed, but we understood the thinking.

Occasionally a large venue calls for subtlety. That is why, when people ask which performance I am most proud of, I cite Pack of Lies, by Hugh Whitemore.

Essentially, this was a fictionalised account of another major news story, this time the infamous 1960s spy case involving the Krogers. The play imagines the position of the family they befriended while the couple supplied state secrets to the Russians. It is ingenious in concept, clever in construction and provides powerful character parts.

Our production arrived at the De La Warr Pavilion in 1992. Director June Jenkins cast it strongly throughout. The line-up included newspaper colleague Paul Siegert as Kroger (Paul later became a skilled political journalist on BBC TV). As rehearsals unfolded, there was a feeling this was going to be something special. The chemistry seemed spot on.

As the husband / father of the family portrayed, I was required to provide the moving postscript to the story following the eventual arrest of the friends who had lived a lie.

It consisted of a full page and a half monologue that called for varied pace, nuances and restrained emotion as I revealed that my character's wife, played splendidly by trusty campaigner Elsie Wright, had died as a result of the strain of discovering the shocking truth.

As always, the fear of failure ruled. Mess this up, Elms, I told myself, and you'll be too embarrassed ever to go on stage again. Well, I didn't mess up.

The whole team had been in stunningly good form and my final soliloquy left hardly a dry eye in the house. I must have rehearsed that last page and a half of dialogue privately a hundred times yet I knew the slightest lapse in concentration could ruin it.

Being ultra self-critical, my chief emotion afterwards was one of relief. As I left the stage after the last of four performances, one of the crew said to me: "Are you all right?" It was then that I realised I had tears rolling down my face.

Relief, indeed.

Considerably less than subtle was Dangerous Obsession, an N. J. Crisp play we did under our new name, Rother Theatre Company. It called for me to fire a gun across the stage and shoot the glass out of a character's hand. The gun was a theatrical device, akin to a starting pistol. The glass was an ingenious sugar-based prop that could be easily crushed on cue. Concerned pavilion security staff came running when they heard the gun blast at dress rehearsal.

And on the opening night, our 'deaf old lady in the back row' didn't miss it, either.

Embarrassingly, that production was memorable for another reason. An actor's wrong cue during the Friday performance led to a chunk of script being omitted, including some vital plot information. By the time the error was spotted we were unable to talk ourselves back on track. The audience went home fifteen minutes early, hopefully none the wiser.

A change of direction brought one of my biggest theatrical challenges. It followed the death of Diana, Princess of Wales in 1997.

Bexhill's own Deputy Lieutenant, Ivor Brampton, took it upon himself to book the De La Warr Pavilion for a tribute concert, which would raise money for the newly set-up memorial fund. We ran a story about it in the Bexhill Observer.

I spoke to Ivor that Friday night, wished him well with the project and said if I could do anything to help don't hesitate to ask. He fairly snatched my hand off.

"Can you come and see me in the morning?" he enquired. I could and we met for coffee.

Ivor, importantly, had set machinery in motion but he hoped that by utilising my know-how and theatrical contacts I could make the production happen ... in just four weeks! He had already secured the services of operatic tenor Andrew MacKenzie-Wicks (son of a former Bexhill mayor) and the renowned Janice Blake Dance Studio. A great start.

By the time the second cup of coffee was finished the outline of the show was in place and I had suggested a number of quality acts of my acquaintance that I could approach. By the end of the day we had the Bexhill Light Operatic and Dramatic Society (BLODS) on board plus the BATS. I arranged for my group, Rother Theatre Company, to provide the backstage requirement.

Things were moving. Through a web of contacts, I put together a show that I thought would have broad appeal to a Bexhill audience. Of course, a concert in Diana's name was always going to fill the pavilion, so it was doubly important to ensure quality. Merely trading on the cause would have been dishonest.

Music, song and dance were the essential ingredients. I scoured Bexhill and Hastings venues, seeking suitable talent and made more than 100 phone calls. No-one turned me down, so I could hand-pick the talent I wanted to create the right blend. It was hard work but, my goodness, what an indulgence!

The plan was to give the show a light opening and work towards a more classical finish, while signing up top notch front-of-curtain acts such as the Bexhill Harmony ladies chorus and accordionist Lourdes Madigasekera to enable continuity during set changes.

From pop band Posh through to the Bexhill Big Band, Teck Quartet and top-of-the-bill Andrew MacKenzie Wicks, everyone was disciplined, stuck to their scheduled time limit and thoroughly deserved the generous audience response. Veteran compere John Woodhams held the whole production together in engaging style.

The only gripe I received from any of the proposed acts had come from within my own household when my then 16-year-old pianist daughter Sarah said: "I wondered when you were going to invite me ..."

I didn't want to be accused of nepotism but her performance of a self-penned tune called The Island (in deference to Princess Diana's final resting place) justified the risk. Classically trained schoolgirl pianist Jennifer Clark played with great confidence during her stint at the pavilion's Steinway.

Public response suggested the hard work had been thoroughly worth while. Actors Roger Moore and Dudley Moore and England goalkeeper David Seaman had been among those to send goodwill messages. And we learned that, at around 1,000 people, the Diana gala had posted a record-breaking pavilion audience for a multi-act show.

I was so pleased for Ivor that his initiative had led to a memorial fund cheque of more than £5,000 being presented. A thank-you letter from Kensington Palace graces my souvenir album.

The gala's success persuaded me to pursue an idea I had been wrestling with for a few years: to stage a Christmas-themed show at the pavilion. So in 1998 I gambled on privately hiring the theatre and presenting Season's Greetings, utilising local talent and highlighting each half with White Christmas and Silent Night tableaux.

Again, I had fantastic help and co-operation from all involved, including my trusty sidekick Ian Fishwick, whose backstage skills and energy were paramount. Numbers attending were not quite of Diana proportions but costs were cleared and £1,500 donated to local causes.

The success of that venture led to a visiting producer asking me to serve as consultant to a charity show at Eastbourne a few weeks later. Several of our stars reprised their acts and I made a guest appearance as Father Christmas, walking across a crowded stage to give Susan Maughan a peck on the cheek after she'd sung her trademark song, Bobby's Girl.

And so it was back to more familiar territory, treading the boards. My appearances were becoming fewer and the jibes about making more comebacks than Sinatra were frequent.

A great personal joy was that all five of our children would be actively involved in the theatre group and all showing considerable flair.

Our eldest, Juliet, then 12, played in Frederick Knott's thriller, Wait Until Dark, while Sarah and Mark, without influence from their parents, were chosen to play brother and sister in Henry James' supernatural drama, The Turn of the Screw. That production proved something of a family coup with Barbara playing the housekeeper.

In his early teens, Matthew provided valuable set-building input for us, only to display latent acting skills during his college years. Victoria, our youngest, stubbornly vowed never to get involved after being brought up in a household full of theatre talk. She finally succumbed, aged ten, by reading a children's story during our Victorian Christmas tour.

That completed a third generation of amateur theatrical involvement since Barbara's parents, Reg and Mary, had also been prominent participants. A strong family bond remained central to our lives, never more so than during one extraordinary decade of contrasts.

At Christmas 1980 we lost our daughter Catherine at birth. Two years later Barbara's brother Peter was cut down by cancer at 47. The same cruel disease took Reg in 1984, Mary in 1986 and my mother in 1989.

And yet during the same decade we could celebrate the safe arrival of four of our children into the world ... all this while gainfully employed at the newspaper and fully involved with the theatre troupe.

What turned out to be my last stage performance took place in 2001. I played the ship's steward in a pleasingly powerful production of Sutton Vane's vintage drama, Outward Bound.

This wonderfully eerie piece of theatre was well received by playgoers as the pavilion stage was transformed into a floating bar-lounge. The essential story tells of a random group of passengers sailing off to who-knows-where for reasons unexplained. Surely, someone was trying to tell me something.

It seemed amazing that after all those years of on and off-stage dramas not one performance had to be cancelled due to illness or worse. I remember thinking, too, how lucky I had been to survive a long newspaper career with just four days off sick.

Little did I realise what was waiting for me in the wings...

Spot the difference: A mere 60 years separate these photographs of Philip Elms. Below: Elms, the young film critic, meets Hollywood legend Ann-Margret on a promotional trip to London in 1971. The star's attention is momentarily taken by cinema manager Leslie Cragg.

A promotional display for a BATS production of The Peacocks Must Go. Matinee idol Elms is centre, left, with future wife Barbara bottom, left. The scene picture - taken for the Bexhill Observer by Jimmy Burke - shows Elms slouching on the sofa in his amateur theatrical debut. The play, Silver Wedding, was staged at the De La Warr Pavilion in 1966. Below, Elms meets his musical hero, Four Seasons legend Bob Gaudio, and his lovely wife, Judy Parker Gaudio.

Barbara has put up with me for the best part of four decades. We played man and wife on stage before we did it for real. Right: An unposed picture (honestly) at my Hastings Observer desk in 1970. Below: A big moment in 1966 when the Queen and Prince Philip finally got to meet L. J. Bartley, editor of the Bexhill Observer.

6 A friendly jar

MY personal experience of hospitals had been largely divided into three categories: Having my tonsils out at aged eight, dutifully supporting my wife during childbirth and assorted visits.

All that was to be supplemented big time in the winter of 2002, yet I was still able to break a major news story.

Office colleagues must have become irritated by my persistent coughing. They said I should take myself home. As it fell during one of my turns of duty as acting editor, I felt I could not simply walk away and leave others in the lurch. They didn't quite see it that way: "Go on, bugger off; the papers will still come out."

Things must have been bad because I took their advice.

I became progressively more uncomfortable over the next few days and visited a duty GP that weekend. His diagnosis was "Chest infection with possible pneumonia." He prescribed tablets to be taken daily for seven days. Although I had little difficulty breathing I found the combination of lying down and breathing to be problematic.

As I sat in an armchair, unable to eat or sleep for a week, I discovered for the first time how long 24 hours really is (and not a single track repeated on Classic FM). Barbara kept an eye on me as well as working for the Employment Service, sorting the house and doing the school run.

Clearly, the tablets were not working. My condition worsened and I started hallucinating. My GP summoned an ambulance to get me into hospital. Once on board, a paramedic checked the oxygen levels in my lungs.

"What should the levels be?" I remember asking.

"In a man of your age about 94 per cent," she said.

"What readings are you getting?" I enquired.

"Eighty-three per cent in your right lung, eleven per cent in your left."

Pumped up with oxygen for the nine-mile journey, I arrived at the Conquest Hospital in Hastings to find scenes bordering on the chaotic. The assessment unit overflowed with patients needing attention. A bed was eventually found for me there and a duty doctor set to work.

Impressively, he made a speedy assessment of my condition and started to drip-feed antibiotics into my left arm. Nurses regularly checked temperature and blood pressure.

The overcrowding of hospitals was making national headlines and, like countless others at Hastings, no ward could be found for me. The assessment unit became so busy that doctors had no choice but to sit on the end of my bed to tend other patients lying on beds and trolleys in corridors.

It was five days before a ward could be found to accommodate me. But apart from the Piccadilly Circus aspect, I had no complaint about the treatment I was receiving.

Professional opinion simplified was that I had contracted one germ on the back of another. The result was a rare and virulent form of pneumonia with emphysema thrown in for good measure. X-rays revealed the full shocking extent of the problem. A vast quantity of fluid had formed in the left lung cavity. Fortunately, the right lung was largely untouched.

Medics admitted they'd never seen anything like it. For several days doctors, nurses and students would gaze in wonderment at the X-ray picture repeatedly attached to the light box. It proved a prelude to a presentation on my case in the lecture theatre.

Clearly the fluid had to be removed. A four-strong medical team gathered at my bedside. Local anaesthetic was administered and a hole bored through the left side of my ribcage. Sensing it was an uncomfortable experience, a female student doctor held my hand in reassurance.

Less reassuring was the comment of the medic trying to insert a frighteningly wide tube: "You have one of the toughest ribcages I've come across," he said as he accepted the challenge with good humoured relish.

The tube was inserted, attached to a large jar on the floor (the jar would become my closest companion for the next three weeks). Suddenly there was a whoosh and the fluid hit the litre mark on the jar within seconds.

"Where did that come from?" My crass question required no answer.

An emergency occurred a few days later when the tube flew out of my lung cavity under pressure, exposing a gaping hole in my side. I cried out for help. Staff came running and a senior nurse plugged the hole with his thumb to prevent infection while medics were summoned to apply more robust stitching.

My foodless, sleepless existence lasted eleven days in all. I lost three-stone. The continued draining of the fluid (some two and a half litres eventually) meant I could lie down again.

I felt, too, if I could make the effort to shave off the ridiculous beard I had grown in dreary shades of grey I might pose a less hideous sight to my family, friends and colleagues on visits.

Aware of the effect my predicament must be having on Barbara and the children, I tried to conserve energy to enable me to play the cheery father when they came to see me.

Definite progress seemed to be made over the next two weeks. So I was slightly taken aback when my consultant said he'd been speaking to a colleague about my case and would like him to see me.

"How would you feel about going to Guy's Hospital?"

I replied: "If that's where you think I should be, then fine."

An ambulance crew arrived to take me to London. A senior nurse rang Barbara and I scarcely had time to say goodbye to Keith, a fellow patient I had befriended.

A Royal Naval veteran and long-term patient suffering chronic lung problems, Keith had taken a liking to my Andrea Bocelli CD, Sacred Arias, so we gave him a copy as a farewell gift. We had filled the men's ward with operatic-style music; the women, apparently, preferred rock 'n' roll.

As far as I was aware, this was no emergency but the ambulance driver seemed to cover the 70-mile journey at a fair lick. I could see little through the darkened windows but became aware that we had turned onto a garage forecourt close to our destination. "Even an ambulance needs petrol," I reasoned.

"It's not that," said the attendant. "The driver's sat-nav has broken down, so he has had to pull in to get directions through a tricky one-way system."

As I was stretchered into the renowned London hospital it was wonderful to feel the breeze and a few drops of rain, a simple and previously unappreciated joy denied me during my 16 days at the Conquest.

My ward at Guy's seemed like an aircraft hangar compared to the Conquest. It could not disguise its Dickensian origins and I half expected to be serenaded by the cast of Oliver! The room contained more men attached to tubes and jars than you could shake a stethoscope at.

Barbara, herself diagnosed with acute anxiety due to my illness, made the first of several train journeys to be with me. At my request she brought a fleece for me to wear to offset the March draught whistling through the cavernous ward.

Temperature and blood pressure checks confirmed both remained high. Daily X-rays meant waiting up to 90 minutes for a porter to push my wheelchair back to the ward. Shortage of staff was blamed.

One dutiful porter was apologetic: "They're not dedicated, that's the problem. If they think they can get as much money on the dole, they just don't bother turning up for work. It's terrible."

Over the next few days - a large jar still my special friend - I saw two of the leading heart and lung experts in the country (happily, my heart was deemed to be strong).

One quietly explained the fluid had forced my left lung out of position. One option was to perform 'serious surgery' and return the lung to its rightful place with the aid of a 'sugary glue.' Another was to leave things alone and trust nature to do the surgeon's dirty work. The second option was chosen, much to my relief. A tentative time-slot in the operating theatre that Thursday morning was cancelled.

Temperature and blood pressure were slowly returning to normal and as eating habits increased so did my weight. I passed the time sitting quietly and reading Alec Guinness' autobiography, Blessings in Disguise.

His often understated style of acting had always appealed to me and his life story was illuminating, ranging from gentle domesticity to grand pomposity. I needed to know, also, that I had the staying power to read chapter after chapter; my physical frailty at the Conquest had turned even a single paragraph into an ordeal.

For an occasional change of scenery, my jar and I would take a stroll to the main staircase, pausing to gaze enviously at people walking in the streets below; it seemed such a long time since I had enjoyed that basic freedom.

One other check had to be carried out before discharge: would my energy levels allow me to negotiate the dozen stairs we had at home? A health visitor suggested she took me to practise on the hospital staircase.

"Don't worry," I said. "I tried out the hospital staircase yesterday."

"How many stairs did you manage?" she enquired, slightly alarmed at my unaccompanied adventure.

"Forty-two."

The practise exercise was abandoned.

Easter was approaching and, knowing what a busy time that was in the Elms household, I discouraged visitors, preferring that ecclesiastic obligations went ahead without interruption. I was content to sit up in bed counting my blessings.

A radio proved invaluable company. The Spurs v. Middlesbrough commentary on Radio Five that Saturday afternoon was interrupted by the announcement of the Queen Mother's death at the age of 101.

Removing my earpiece, I adopted journalistic mode to share the news with fellow patients and their visitors. If anyone thought these were the ramblings of a deranged patient who'd forgotten to take his medication, my story was confirmed by the pictures now appearing on the TV at the nurses' station.

I was discharged from Guy's on Easter Day and my good friend Ian kindly drove Barbara to London to collect me. Follow-up care suggested I was on the mend, even if my reduced lung power would remain. I was still three months away from more familiar news presentation but at least the disruption to home life that this sort of thing inevitably causes had begun to subside.

The whole experience was starkly summed up following a chance meeting. A source close to my predicament said: "We were very worried about you, especially as it was touch and go at one point."

Some weeks later I bumped into my friendly tube-wielding doctor in a Conquest corridor. He informed me the lecture theatre session had been a big success. I said I was glad to have been of benefit to the medical profession.

I was on my way to see my former ward buddy Keith who said plans were being made to transfer him to a Cheshire Home after seven months in hospital. I wished him well and promised I would visit. He died before I could fulfil that promise.

7 Stage presence

IT is probably no coincidence that my dual interests of newspapers and theatre have dovetailed so conveniently. The similarities are clear. One is a representation of real life, the other thinks it is but is really an illusion. The only issue is deciding which is which.

Perhaps my best acting has been done offstage. A certain level of performance can be beneficial when dealing with real-life characters showing a range of emotions from the despair of a bereaved parent to the unbounded joy of a lottery winner. Possibly theatre is one step closer to reality ... at least the parameters are clearly defined.

One real-life performance was required on a multi-sports reporting trip to Dordrecht in Holland where local teams took on their Hastings counterparts.

The Dutch and British contingents sprang a surprise 21st birthday party for me ... music, dancing, presentations. They really made a fuss of me. The only problem was that it was actually my 22nd birthday.

Someone had overheard a reference to my pending birthday and got the wrong end of the stick. What could I do? I just played along with the celebration and the embarrassing truth was never revealed.

Meeting people who make their living from performing in public has always been a fascination of mine, especially if they write or compose their own material (I'm just glad I have never had to sing my copy to anyone!). Indeed, working for newspapers enabled me to meet a range of celebrities.

An early memory comes from the mid-60s when I was invited backstage to meet Johnny Speight. He was in Bexhill to record a TV show. Johnny had become firmly established by creating and writing the Alf Garnett comedy series, Till Death Us Do Part, the No 1 rated show on BBC Television at the time.

He enthralled and amazed a packed dressing room by rattling off dialogue at extraordinary pace. I reckoned it must take him half an hour to write a 30-minute episode. "Pretty much," the lovable Cockney replied through his rasping trademark chuckle. The Garnett saga - with a little help from character actor Warren Mitchell - brought Johnny Speight an amazing success late in life, an inspiration for us all, perhaps.

My youthful days on the Hastings Observer sparked the suggestion that I should write a young people's column. I wanted to launch it with a blockbuster article and was lucky enough to get an exclusive interview with Roy Orbison in London in 1969.

It was not intended to be exclusive but by the time my companion and I had found the stage door of the Hammersmith Odeon the post-concert Press call was over.

Would the American recording legend still see us? The lone security man took our ID and disappeared inside. *We've got no chance*, we thought. The lone security man returned. "Come with me," he said. *We were in.* We spent ten minutes in the company of Roy Orbison and his new German-born bride, Barbara, whom he had met in a Leeds nightclub.

Roy's songs had played an important part during my growing up. From the despair of It's Over (a record I recall playing twenty-seven times the day I bought it) to the encouragement of future fulfilment in Oh Pretty Woman, there was plenty of scope for exercising my lungs as I walked from my first block release course to my Harlow digs.

It struck me that if a lot had happened in my life over the previous four years, it was nothing compared to Roy Orbison's tragic experiences. His first wife Claudette had died in a motorcycle accident. Then two sons perished in a house fire. Yet here he was ... still in his early 30s, remarried, on stage in England and performing heartbreak songs such as Only the Lonely and In Dreams.

Seldom have I met a star with so much confidence in his own ability. No matter how often he performed his most popular songs his simple philosophy was similar to that of a good actor ... it must sound like the first time every time. Roy created not only a style but a persona. He was an absolute gentleman, his death at 52 a crying shame.

A regrettable postscript to this is that my world exclusive interview with Roy Orbison never saw the light of day. Editor John Cornelius was utterly baffled by the title I wanted to give to the new young people's feature.

I assured him that Alive and Well was a hip expression of the day and that young people would relate to it. I refused to go with something pathetic like Youth Chat or Youth Notes.

Eventually, the editor exercised his absolute right to cancel the project.

Through a tie-up with the management of the Hastings cinema, I was soon able to meet a Hollywood star. Ann-Margret had previously played opposite Elvis Presley in Viva Las Vegas and was described as the only co-star to equal him in musical talent and sexual charisma.

The Swedish-born actress was in London in 1971 to promote her latest film to the British Press. She was co-starring with Jack Nicholson, Candice Bergen and Art Garfunkel in Carnal Knowledge. Ann-Margret's drive and comic timing impressed the critics (not least the youthful reviewer from downtown Hastings).

She looked sensational and not just because she was going to be photographed with me in a mock library setting. I might have said "I almost didn't recognise you with clothes on" but I resisted. She smiled demurely and answered the most inane questions that the Hastings Observer representative could throw at her.

It's been good to say hello to comedy icons Kenneth Horne and Eddie Izzard and actor / playwright Derek Benfield (especially as I had been involved in a couple of his plays, Murder for the Asking and Touch and Go).

I also much enjoyed a quiet coffee with pianist Russ Conway. I was involved with Bexhill Theatre Supporters Club when Russ accepted an invitation to open our summer fayre on the terrace of the De La Warr Pavilion and promote his up-coming show at the civic theatre.

Shortly before he succumbed to cancer in 2000, Russ told me of the joy he still derived from belting out trademark hits like Side Saddle, Roulette and China Tea. Honky tonk tunes like these made him the biggest selling UK recording artiste of 1959 and he went on to sustain his career for more than four decades. His composing, including some more 'serious' music, virtually ran as a parallel career under his real name, Trevor Stanford.

Yet he revealed a secret regret. When elderly ladies said they'd just bought his Greatest Hits he rued the legal stranglehold his record company had kept over him. Thus he collected something like an old penny for each record sold, a rate never reviewed over the years.

Covering sport brought me into contact with a host of further household names who climbed to the top of their professions. World darts king Keith Deller and snooker favourites Terry Griffiths and Cliff Thorburn were among those who helped to steer their pursuits out of the public bars and into the theatres and on to television.

Controlled aggressors like football legends Ted Drake and Alan Ball and cricket's Colin Cowdrey also knew the value of discipline. It seemed to me that a cool head and tight discipline were qualities I would most covet in the mad, mad world of newspapers.

If sometimes it was necessary to throw a metaphorical punch or two, I could always blame the example of another legend I met, Henry Cooper. A charming man of the people if ever there was one. Not that you had to be a boxer to indulge in a spot of sparring. I once provided the warm-up act at a sports dinner to former Scotland international and Manchester United manager Tommy Docherty.

"I've always had a soft spot for journalists," he told our audience. "It's at the bottom of my garden."

A London pub was the unlikely setting for a meeting in 2008 with another iconic figure of the American entertainment industry.

Screenwriter Marshall Brickman had won an Oscar for writing Annie Hall with Woody Allen. He was already the proud holder of a Lifetime Achievement Award from the

Writers' Guild of America when he agreed to meet an international group of devotees of the music of Frankie Valli and the Four Seasons.

The occasion was the West End launch of Jersey Boys, the award-laden musical play of the Seasons' life story he had co-scripted with rookie Rick Elice to Broadway acclaim. The pub opposite the Prince Edward Theatre was doing roaring late afternoon trade. Imagine my surprise when I returned from a quick visit to the toilet to be greeted with an outstretched hand and a voice saying: "Hello, I'm Marshall Brickman ..."

What else could I say but "Hello, I'm Philip Elms?"

Marshall and Rick were engaging company and truly humbled by our support for the Jersey Boys project. Great though it was to meet them, the journalist in me chalked this up as a missed opportunity. I would love to have conducted a proper interview with Marshall.

Here was a true giant of the US leisure industry. *Talk to me about Sleeper, Manhattan, the soundtrack of Deliverance, the writing of Jersey Boys!* But here we were in a small, noisy bar less than an hour away from the red carpet parade of stars. Time and circumstance were against me yet memories remain of a surreal experience.

Through it all one international celebrity remained elusive to me - until later that night when I tracked him down at the most unlikely of venues ...

8 Music for all Seasons

FOR longer than I have been a journalist, the music of the Four Seasons has been important to me. Vivaldi may have been similarly drawn but that's another story. The Four Seasons who provided the soundtrack to my career are the Italian / American quartet who moved from the clubs of New Jersey to the recording studios of New York and a global audience.

The original line-up of Frankie Valli, Bob Gaudio, Tommy Devito and Nick Massi produced ground-breaking songs such as Sherry, Walk Like Man and Rag Doll and were enrolled in the Rock and Roll Hall of Fame in 1990. In the 21st century their warts-and-all life story, Jersey Boys, was put on stage to vast critical and popular acclaim on Broadway, in the West End and around the world.

Colleagues had to do no head scratching in choosing a parting gift when I switched from the Bexhill Observer to the Hastings title in 1968. They presented me with Edizione d'Oro, a double album of Seasons hits.

The group enjoyed a 1970s resurgence thanks to titles like The Night, Who Loves You and December 1963 (Oh, What a Night) and by the time I met Frankie Valli at the Dome Theatre, Brighton, in 1992 the group had been rebranded as Frankie Valli and the Four Seasons.

The diminutive lead singer with a three-and-a-half octave voice range was happy to chat. He took quite a shine to my then 10-year-old daughter Sarah and told her: "Have a wonderful life, sweety."

I reminded her of that line as she prepared to join Sussex Police in 2009. She gave me one of her looks which suggested I was the one who needed the knife-proof vest.

Through linking up with fellow Seasonites across the United States and Europe, I have developed a depth of knowledge (some family members would call it an obsession) about the music, life and times of the Four Seasons.

Yet I harboured an unfulfilled wish for the best part of half a century. I wanted to meet Bob Gaudio, original Season, songwriting genius and production guru. I needed to track him down (though not in a stalking sense, you understand).

The seeds of a remarkable career were sown back in the 1940s when a life so genteel and middle class was anything but the norm in Bergenfield, New Jersey.

Displaying a talent and confidence beyond his years, Robert Gaudio emerged as a piano prodigy when he wowed audiences at New York's Carnegie Hall at the tender age of seven, though these days he cannot remember the piece of music he played.

Probably his biggest achievement over the next decade was staying out of trouble. Street crime was rife, many a destiny for boys of his age shaped by The Mob.

That he should not only emerge unscathed but carve out a career as one of the most iconic musicians of 20th century popular culture is testimony to the drive and impeccable skills of this quiet, unassuming man.

Musician, singer, songwriter, producer ... Bob Gaudio was described as the quintessential music maker when he was inducted into the prestigious Songwriters Hall of Fame, a few years after entering the Rock and Roll Hall of Fame. So my quest to meet the man behind the legend (not to mention his lovely wife, Judy) took in my home county of East Sussex, an Atlantic crossing to New York and back to London over the course of three decades.

It was in 1958 that a 15-year-old kid with an ear for a tune wrote a novelty song based around half a dozen different words. Bob Gaudio dropped out of high school in New Jersey to perform Short Shorts with the Royal Teens on tour, sharing a bus with Buddy Holly, Chuck Berry, Jackie Wilson and the Everly Brothers.

At 19 he disassembled the score of the Bruce Channel song, Hey Baby, and turned it into another minimalist offering, Sherry, for his new group, the Four Seasons. Sherry provided the catalyst not only for the longevity of the Four Seasons but for a diverse and award-laden career.

The list of artistes to benefit from Gaudio's work reads like a Who's Who of American late 20th century music: Frank Sinatra to Frankie Valli; Barbra Streisand to Diana Ross; Neil Diamond to Michael Jackson. Long-time collaborator Bob Crewe summed up Gaudio's prime quality: "He understands harmonic structure."

No accurate figure exists to illustrate sales of singles and albums bearing the performing or production stamp of Bob Gaudio but 200 million would be a conservative estimate.

My peculiar interest in the life and times of Bob Gaudio is fuelled chiefly by the distinctive and developing sound of the Four Seasons. Yet here was the man who sat down at the piano at the age of 24 and composed the standard, Can't Take My Eyes Off You, a song recorded by more than 200 artistes and the fifth most played song on American radio in the 20th century with 8 million plays.

The more I heard, read and discussed with like-minded devotees around the world, the more I wanted to meet the man. And not just because I considered I had contributed greatly to his fortune.

I tried my luck when the Seasons played Eastbourne's Congress Theatre in the mid-70s. Gaudio had travelled even though he wasn't performing with the band at the time. Alas, security intervened; Mr Gaudio was seeing no-one.

Undeterred, I hung around for a few decades. Another door opened with the emergence of Jersey Boys.

I flew to New York in 2007 both to see the show and in the hope that a certain Mr Gaudio would be on the scene. A six-hour lunch with Seasonally-connected chums brought the shock revelation that Gaudio was currently in London, making arrangements for the West End version of the show.

The good news was that I was invited to a Broadway cast party that Sunday night and that Bob Gaudio would be there! The bad news was my plane left for home the day before. Was this guy trying to avoid me?

Patient to a fault, I waited for the 2008 West End opening to seize my best chance yet. By then I had my good friend Charles

Alexander on board. Charles is a distinguished New York journalist, confidante to the Four Seasons Partnership and associate producer of Jersey Beat, a 2007 CD / DVD box set of Seasons music. Charles had secured for Barbara and me VIP invitations to join the celebrity throng at the London launch night party.

We were bussed from the Prince Edward Theatre to the impressive surroundings of London's Natural History Museum. Cast and creative team were among hundreds already assembled; Queen guitarist Brian May, West End troupers Elaine Paige and Russ Abbott, and songstress Cilla Black joined in ... lights, orchestra, theatrical chatter.

Among cast members I was privileged to meet was the talented Stephen Ashfield who plays the Bob Gaudio character in Jersey Boys. But not even a darkened corner could hide the presence of the tall, slender, grey-haired figure of the man, himself.

Ever at his side was the vivacious redhead I deemed to be the woman Bob Gaudio always introduces as 'my lovely wife.' While the great man chatted to a friend, I approached Judy Parker and greeted her by name. She seemed pleasantly surprised that someone in faraway England knew who she was. I told her I was well aware of the vital contribution she had made to the Four Seasons' revival in the '70s.

"Thank-you," she said. "I was just glad to be allowed to do it."

Among other songs, Judy had written the lyrics to December 1963 (Oh What a Night), a poetically lurid account of Bob's sexual initiation (with someone else). It was at one time the biggest US chart hit in Billboard history and, of course, features prominently in Jersey Boys.

I said I'd followed her husband's career with great interest. She attracted his attention.

"Bob, this is Phil."

"Hi," he proferred.

Suddenly I was shaking hands with Bob Gaudio.

Yes, he was absolutely delighted with his British cast, headed by Ryan Malloy, Stephen Ashfield, Glenn Carter and Philip Bulcock.

"I think they're wonderful, as good as any cast we have," he told me. "Their accents are very New Jersey and the Prince Edward is a perfect setting."

Unlike his business partner, Frankie Valli, Gaudio is not a showman by inclination. Essentially shy, he was nevertheless impressed when I produced a copy of David Cote's lavish book of the Jersey Boys story (foreword written by Charles). I had spotted it at the Virgin store in Manhattan, a must-have at $40.

It includes an historic photograph of Gaudio's manuscript scribblings of the song he originally called Cheri but later morphed into the iconic Sherry.

"I found it in his father's loft," chipped in Judy.

I have never been an autograph hunter but Bob and Judy agreed to overlay the manuscript with their signatures.

So there it was: from hearing Sherry for the first time to meeting its composer, a mere 46 years had elapsed ... my quest to meet a music legend (and his lovely wife) fulfilled in the unlikely setting of the Natural History Museum.

The biggest challenge remained for my long suffering wife: how to take a commemorative photograph of two men in black suits, black shirts and black ties, standing in a darkened corner at midnight. Happily, she got a result with the help of a little computer enhancement.

Oh, what a night!

9 Final curtain

OUT there in the big, wide world the new Millennium ushered in a fresh era of hopes and fears: hopes for family health and prosperity; fears that terrorism would take an even firmer hold on the news agenda.

The year 2001 brought one of the gravest atrocities perpetrated on the human race. Yet while New York was being attacked from the sky and global politics would get its biggest wake-up call for more than half a century, events were running their course at a personal level, too.

The serious illness I contracted early in 2002 had a major impact on my energy levels. Preparing for plays is a demanding pursuit and, even if I negotiated that aspect, I knew that once in front of an audience I'd never be heard by the deaf old lady in the back row.

I reckoned I owed it to my family – not to mention my patient employers - to channel the energy where it was most needed. And so the curtain fell on my stage career after 35 fascinating years.

Times were changing fast for local newspapers, too. A steady decline in weekly sales showed no sign of abating. The Hastings Observer was averaging a healthy 26,240 copies per week in 1974. When I rejoined the paper as sports editor in 1979, the average weekly sale was down to 24,627.

By the time I left the business in 2009 we were struggling to hit 19,000 (a decline in sales not entirely down to me!).

Newspapers always like to emphasise the number of readers they attract by multiplying the sales figure by 2.5. Somehow, then, we managed to ship around 14,000 readers. Sadly, local newspapers were no longer essential reading. Long gone are the days when our products were considered papers of record, that is, if it happened it was reported.

Glance at the newspaper archive and you will witness a tantalising snapshot of life in the community. These days that snapshot would be rather less revealing, assuming that such an archive still exists. Minimal staffing levels render such lofty ideals impossible to maintain. My window cleaner, in an unsolicited observation, put it this way: "It's all pictures and crime these days."

Papers continued to strive for strong advertising revenue from the property, motoring and job recruitment markets and these were devastated by the deepest of recessions less than a decade into the 21st century.

With nearly seven out of ten of potential readers having internet access, it was no surprise that businesses chose to spend their advertising budgets more wisely than ever before. The trend to develop customised websites became all-consuming. Internet links opened up boundless possibilities. Shopping on line was fun, easy and phenomenally popular.

Newspapers, too, saw an opportunity to attract website revenue although many advertisers remained unconvinced in matters of impact and viewing numbers. Exposure on a paper's website could not compare with a print display, they argued. The dilemma for newspapers was how to attract advertising to both print and online strands from a fast-shrinking market place.

The obvious hook to attract advertisers was to provide a rolling news service that, theoretically, would encourage likely customers to log on several times a day. All too easily, papers fell into the trap of providing a free round-the-clock news service, while endeavouring to sell identical material in print at the end of the week.

Ideally, breaking news on the website would be followed up in the paper with analysis and background. Staffing levels were simply inadequate to supply a separate, complementary service, so readers had a choice: enjoy a free on-demand service or wait until the end of the week and pay close to 50p for it.

The initial argument that a web service would not impact on the paper seemed a desperate expression of hope over reality. It defied all logic.

Lifestyles were changing. Businesses had more pressing concerns than how to find the money to place an ad with the local paper. Newspapers could respond or pay the price. Publicly, proprietors were reacting to the economic challenges of the day. Privately, they knew the game was almost up. Share prices plunged. Restructuring became the buzzword. Journalists' jobs were culled on an unprecedented scale. Not even editors were spared.

In our small corner of the world the ominous signs became more numerous throughout 2008 (and not just because we were into our seventh managing director in less than five years). The downturn in property, motors and jobs revenue accelerated alarmingly. A senior sub-editor walked out over falling standards. She was not replaced. A reporter moved on. She was not replaced, either. This from a team already severely depleted in strength.

During the first week of December, 2008, our managing director, Steve Clark, solemnly informed staff that salary reviews were being 'deferred' for six months as a result of the credit crunch and economic recession.

Deferred had become a favourite company euphemism. It suggested jam tomorrow and stopped the natives from getting restless. No-one was fooled.

Only two months earlier Steve had spoken to me about my own situation, aware that I had voiced the notion that I would welcome retirement some way short of my 65th birthday. He was trying to avoid imposing hurt elsewhere during cost-conscious times.

Certainly I had some serious thinking to do, having reached the big Six-O the previous summer. Did I want to soldier on for another five years of long, pressurised days, wrestling with creaking technology and with job satisfaction (not to mention the industry itself) in rapid decline? Not really.

We were counting down to a massive implosion. Stress levels rose as standards fell. Pagination was kept artificially high in relation to both the advertising revenue and the generation of editorial copy by a hard-working but depleted team.

Readers were encouraged to assume that everyone at the Observer was having a ball. Not a word of the paper's problems appeared in print. The tears of the clown were not for public viewing (and I thought my theatrical career was over!). Corners were routinely cut to produce newspapers on time.

At the end of my heart-to-heart conversation with Steve Clark – a man of decency and integrity – I reluctantly told him the proposed severance deal he had pieced together to persuade me to come off the payrole was inadequate. Tempting though it was to perform a one-man version of The Great Escape, the deal fell some way short of the figure I had in mind, a figure that would more accurately equate to my own accrued redundancy package should the MD wish to take that route. He didn't.

Since I was under no obligation to accept the deal on the table, I put forward a counter suggestion. I would commit myself to another two years with the company (casting myself once again as a glutton for punishment). During that period I would vacate my present 'day job' of sub-editing the Bexhill title to transform our flagship paper, the Hastings Observer, into a product fit for the 21st century. It would be a major challenge but one I was ready to accept.

Getting ever more stroppy in my old age, I demanded the freedom to do it my way. I didn't mean to convey arrogance, merely the frustration that a product once eagerly awaited in people's homes was slipping rapidly down the tubes. I was desperate to do something about it.

A debate around the executive table was not required, just a nod in my direction. And it would not take an extra penny from the editorial budget.

Steve liked what I was saying. "That is music to my ears," he smiled. I had already sounded out editor Peter Lindsey about my plan and he was supportive.

In the run-up to Christmas I consulted the shrinking editorial staff. It was important for them to view the paper's immediate future positively despite the gathering clouds of economic gloom.

My message was: Let's take a deep breath, accept we are working in an imperfect environment and try to produce newspapers that we and the town can be proud of. My thoughts on a re-design were received enthusiastically; where once we had a worthy paper, worthy had become dirty word akin to boring.

I had voiced the view to my bosses that the paper had become locked in an '80s timewarp. This was despite the best endeavours of a string of sub-editors, often forced to work within parameters that were both stifling and unnecessary. I wanted to shift creativity from the back seat to the driver's seat. The paper needed to move on to capture the interest of a new generation of readers.

Colleagues offered sound ideas on freshening up the content with a varied and meaningful look at the town beyond the regular diet of murder, rape and pillage. For an example, I set them a challenge by asking how many stories / pictures we had published in the previous year featuring people aged between 20 and 60. The answer was shamefully few. This imbalance in our coverage would be addressed.

I suggested we were turning around the proverbial juggernaut but, hang in there, and the improvements would manifest themselves in the New Year. It was something they could enjoy being part of and, importantly, something the readers might appreciate as the paper became easier on the eye and simpler to navigate.

I would also front some promotional videos for the website, just as I had done for the Bexhill Observer that summer when their emergence on YouTube triggered nearly 2,000 hits.

Alas, even the best laid plans ...

While home life turned to the festive season, our parent company was in anything but celebratory mood. Recession was hurtling our way like an express train and massive debts had to be refinanced in double quick time. City opinion was divided on whether Johnston Press could survive in its current form. At local level MD Steve was out of the door without time for goodbyes.

Myself and two other senior editorial production staff, Russ Perkins and Andrew Bennett, were told our jobs were at risk as a result of major restructuring. My plans to spearhead a new era at the Hastings Observer were consigned to the recycling bin.

Would I accept a revised and less creative production role in a regionalised subbing hub at Horsham (100-mile daily round trip)? No, thank you. My two colleagues reached similar conclusions. I was effectively signing my redundancy papers. Sad, but the alternative was even less appealing. I did not wish to become the journalistic equivalent of a battery hen. I talked it over extensively with Barbara. The proposed role amounted to subbing by committee, a recipe for lowering standards if ever I heard of one.

It was time to go.

The legal paperwork was drawn up. Consultation meetings took place. Boxes were ticked by the dozen. The enormity of the decisions being taken would take time to sink in; after all we still had newspapers to produce. I convinced myself I had chosen the correct route, my dream to revitalise the Hastings Observer finally shattered.

The paper had always held a special place in my heart. Growing up on our council estate in the '50s, the Observer was routinely delivered every Saturday morning. It published a picture of me in 1962 with the story that colleague Andrew Parr and I had become the first St John Ambulance cadets in Hastings to notch up 200 hours of voluntary public duty.

It was while scouring the Situations Vacant columns of the Hastings Observer early in 1964 that my father had spotted the advertisement for a junior reporter to join the Bexhill Observer. "That would interest you," he said with absolutely no anticipation of a career that would span 44 years, six months and sixteen days.

No turning back. Time to hand over the baton.

My mind wandered back to where it had all started for me, a small first floor office in Bexhill-on-Sea, checking out the dead and planning royal bunting.

Under the banner of F. J. Parsons Ltd, the family business was still in the hands of the first of seven owners who would eventually make their presence felt, along with a dozen managing directors, a similar number of editors and seven advertisement managers.

I formally stood down as office fire marshal. In this role I had endeavoured to keep the editorial department free of obvious fire hazards and conduct the staff roll call during fire drills.

I cleared my desk over several days. Correspondence going back six years was binned, a stockpile of emails unceremoniously deleted. Uncaptioned photo files that no-one else would understand were wiped.

A company Journalist of the Year accolade from the '80s was dropped into a bin bag along with a Best Use of Colour (second place) certificate from the '90s.

My most treasured piece of memorabilia was already safely in the goodies cabinet at home: an inscribed shield presented to me by Hastings Lions Club in recognition of 'outstanding service' during my sports editing years.

I fired off some emails of the 'thanks and goodbye' variety and shut down my computer to spare myself the emotion of reading any responses.

Staff gathered to say their goodbyes in a ceremony similar to dozens I had taken part in over the years. Kind words were uttered. A wide acceptance this was the end of an era. Part of the furniture, perhaps, but Pickford's were waiting.

I had rehearsed a clever little speech for just this occasion. Come the moment, I couldn't remember my lines. Probably just as well. I adlibbed my appreciation of the companionship and genuine friendships enjoyed for so long.

The final hour was a choker. Going to the gallows must have been something like this, I thought. *Don't get sentimental,* I told myself sternly. But I wasn't listening. I wished colleagues of all departments well and suggested we stayed in touch.

To the younger members of staff, wondering what the future of journalism held, I urged them to stay true to their profession; be assured that every downturn is followed by an upturn and they should be ready with their well-honed skills when that moment arrived.

A final round of handshakes and I was gone.

I was in good company. Apart from Russ and Andrew, lifelong friends and colleagues Ken McEwan and John Dowling, both household names in their patches, had been encouraged to retire several months early.

Ken had spent the last thirty years as sports editor of the Eastbourne Herald series while John had seen out his entire career at the Bexhill Observer from junior reporter to deputy editor.

The three of us mused over the fact that we had all been Bartley Boys, beginning our careers in the same little Bexhill office during the same exciting era of the 1960s. We followed different strands of journalism. Then with almost a century and a half of collective newspaper experience under our belts, we were once again in the same boat, only this time heading for the tunnel marked Exit.

We could feel a book coming on ... but then, who'd want to read it?

Epilogue

L EAVING the newspaper world behind triggered lifestyle changes. Days without deadlines seemed weird. Days of the week became harder to define after the familiar ritual of set functions. Once or twice I was reduced to checking the date on my mobile.

A welcome change was improved sleep patterns; I could go to sleep counting sheep instead of pages. Yet my waking hours still needed to be meaningful aside from putting out the wheelie bins on time and, preferably, on the right day.

My contribution to Three Men and a Quote, I decided, would be written in a disciplined fashion: 10am till 1pm Tuesday to Thursday, the days when I had the house to myself. I could put on a Mozart concerto if I liked, but no sneaking off to watch Sky Sports News. The only interruption, annoyingly, was the string of cold calls offering house insurance.

Post-redundancy family life moved on apace. Our younger son Mark became engaged to Clare; youngest daughter Victoria became engaged to Craig; elder son Matt married Jen; and my father died at 88.

As with all good productions, the possibility of an encore should never be discounted. Sure enough, less than three months after the fond company farewells, I was back in familiar surroundings.

The personnel cutbacks at the Observer group had been so severe it only needed one production staffer to be absent to cause an editorial hiatus. Newly appointed editor-in-chief Keith Ridley asked if I could go back for a couple of weeks to guide the Bexhill Observer through to its print deadline. We negotiated a fee and I agreed to help out. The exercise was repeated several times over the next six months.

Although I always designed the front page myself, most other pages were put together by a subbing pool at Portsmouth who gained access to pages (and the words and pictures I was supplying) via the in-house computer network. For me it was the old job stripped down to bare essentials and minus the deputy management baggage.

It was the first time in the whole of my experience that the company had funded freelance cover in an editorial production crisis. But needs must.

Working again with former colleagues was a joy. But these work interludes were playing havoc with my claims for Job Seekers Allowance. Signing off and signing on again seems a straight forward enough process. If only.

One episode involved a 45-minute form-filling exercise with a distant call centre, an interview so detailed that I was asked if my 61-year-old wife was pregnant. I said if she was I wouldn't be wasting time with this interview, I'd be flogging the story to the world's media.

Not for one moment have I doubted the wisdom of my decision to end my salaried career. I feel liberated and the stress levels have fallen sharply. I am lucky that this major decision in my life was taken after my 60th birthday; less fortunate are colleagues twenty years younger seeking re-employment in a shrinking jobs market.

I am writing a stage play and planning a solo book. My dear wife knows when I'm going to be home. And once that ghastly crab apple tree has come down the front garden will look half decent.

Pass me the chainsaw.